CW00552785

The
LICKEY INCLINE

by
H.C. Casserley

Revised by
Stanley C. Jenkins
BA, Cert. Ed., MA

THE OAKWOOD PRESS

© Oakwood Press 1990

ISBN 0 85361 317 6

First published 1976

Second Edition (revised) 1990

Typeset by Gem Publishing Company, Brightwell, Wallingford, Oxfordshire.

Printed by Alphaprint, Witney, Oxfordshire.

Acknowledgments

I have to acknowledge several sources for information and illustrations which my correspondents have been kind enough to supply towards the preparation of this volume.

First and foremost to my old friend of many years, Harry Daventry, who gladly made available to me details of his astronomical knowledge of early Midland Railway locomotive history, and without which I would certainly not have been able to present as complete a record of the Norris and other engines which worked on the Birmingham & Gloucester, and particularly the Incline itself in earlier years. Also to Mr Brian Reed, whose 'Loco Profile' on Norris engines was additionally most helpful. The line drawing and reproduction of an old painting was reproduced from this volume with his kind permission. And to another old friend, Dr P. Ransome Wallis, for his permission to quote verbatim his account of his entertaining experience on his visit to the Incline in 1950, recounted at the time in *Trains Illustrated*.

Berkhamsted   *H.C. Casserley*
                                                                  October 1975

Published by
The OAKWOOD PRESS
P.O.Box 122, Headington, Oxford.

Contents

Introduction

First published in 1976, *The Lickey Incline* was an unusual addition to the Oakwood range in that it did not deal with a specific line or company history. Instead, it represented an attempt to tell the story of the 2 mile long Lickey Incline in Worcestershire, with a particular emphasis on the many locomotives that have worked over this difficult route since its opening in 1840. The author, H.C. Casserley is a noted historian with a wealth of information at his fingertips, and much of this first-hand experience was incorporated in the text of *The Lickey Incline*, the result being a unique personal *mémoire* that combined anecdote and history in a small but fascinating volume.

By 1989 the original book was long out of print, and when a reprint was being considered it was decided that the original text should be combined with an entirely new selection of photographs to produce a somewhat longer volume. When asked to prepare this new edition I decided to keep Mr Casserley's text in more or less its original form, although one or two new paragraphs have been added. In general, these reflect changes that have taken place since the 1970s, but a little extra information has also been added in relation to the stations at Bromsgrove and Blackwell. It is hoped that readers will approve of the revised text and of the new photographs which have been collected for inclusion in the second edition. Finally, thanks are due to R.J. Essery, and all others who have helped with the preparation of the revised volume.

Witney, Oxfordshire   *Stanley C. Jenkins*
                                                                                              1990

Midland Railway class 2 4–4–0 No. 519 enters Blackwell station with what appears to be an 8-coach train; an 0–6–0T provides banking assistance at the rear.

H.C. Casserley

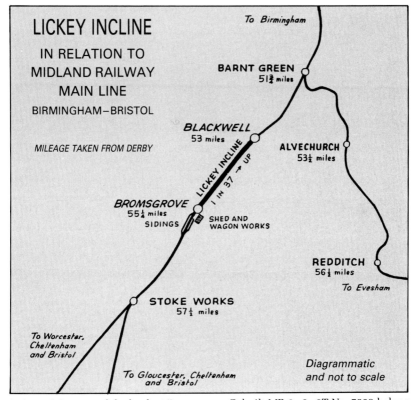

LICKEY INCLINE

IN RELATION TO
MIDLAND RAILWAY
MAIN LINE

BIRMINGHAM–BRISTOL

MILEAGE TAKEN FROM DERBY

To Birmingham

BARNT GREEN
51¾ miles

BLACKWELL
53 miles

LICKEY INCLINE
1 IN 37 → UP

ALVECHURCH
53¼ miles

BROMSGROVE
55¼ miles
SIDINGS

SHED AND
WAGON WORKS

REDDITCH
56¼ miles

To Evesham

STOKE WORKS
57¼ miles

To Worcester,
Cheltenham
and Bristol

To Gloucester, Cheltenham
and Bristol

Diagrammatic
and not to scale

A view of the start of the bank at Bromsgrove. Rebuilt MR 0–6–0T No. 7239 helps a northbound freight up the Incline while a down train is signalled on the southbound line. Note the tools and other signs of activity beside the platelayers' hut; the date is 12th July, 1939. *H.C. Casserley*

A Johnson class 3 4—4—0 No. 776 passes through Blackwell station with a southbound express passenger train.   R.M. Casserley Collection

Part One
The Lickey Incline

My interest in the Lickey Incline goes back a very long way, no less than 70 years. My first acquaintance was when, as a schoolboy, I spent a week's holiday with some distant relations at Barnt Green, where they had a house near the station overlooking the main MR Birmingham–Bristol line. I was already taking a growing interest in railways at that time, to the extent of recording all the engines I saw (I think nearly all of us in those days started that way), but, living in South London, my observations had been chiefly confined to the LSWR, LB&SCR and SECR, with sundry visits to the London main line stations of the railway to the north, particularly St Pancras. The fascination of the Midland started at a very early age and was to continue throughout the years, and notwithstanding the rival claims of many other railways, the MR always remained my first and most enduring love.

Anyway, whilst at Barnt Green I soon found out about the Lickey Incline, not very far away, about which I had only hitherto had some vague knowledge, but where I now spent a good many happy hours by the lineside near the summit at Blackwell. At that time even the famous 0–10–0 No. 2290, later nicknamed 'Big Bertha', had not yet appeared on the scene and the banking duties were almost entirely confined to Johnson 0–6–0Ts.

The fact that I happened quite by chance to be at Derby on New Year's Day 1920, when the new 0–10–0 banking engine made one of its first appearances running trials, and that I was able to secure what was the first photograph of it, apart from possibly official views taken in the works, was of supreme interest to me. Incidentally, I had only just started photography, and had had my first camera for just a fortnight, but managed to secure a good enough picture to have it reproduced in the *Locomotive News* of the time.

Only the vaguest rumours had filtered out as to what the new engine was to be like. Derby was very secretive in those days, and private visits to the works were quite out of the question. When I found that it was actually a ten-coupled engine, only the second this country had ever seen, I am sure I was amazed, to put it mildly, as the Midland had never even had engines with eight-coupled wheels (and never did for that matter, if one excludes the S&DJR 2–8–0s). Knowing that it was intended for banking up the Lickey Incline it naturally enhanced my interest to a very great degree.

These two quite isolated occurrences in my early life, my first acquaintance with the Lickey Incline way back in 1916, and my accidental discovery of No. 2290 on its first public appearance on New Year's Day 1920, and my subsequent interest in these closely related events, make me feel, I hope, qualified to write a short account of this, one of the many interesting sidelines of the story of British railway history in general.

Origins of the Incline

The Lickey Incline, situated on the former LMS route between Birmingham and Bristol, is the steepest to be found on any main line in Great

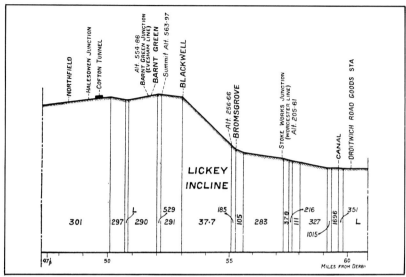

The gradient profile of the section of the Midland Railway Main Line between Droitwich Road and Northfield, which includes the Lickey Incline.

F.J. Dolby's famous painting of the Lickey Incline as it was in the early 1840s with class 'A extra' *Philadelphia* fitted with sandbox on the boiler top. The general surrounding scenery is much the same at the present day; note that the trackwork is laid on longitudinal timber baulks (cross sleepers were however used in cuttings on the Birmingham and Gloucester line).

Britain. With a continuous ascent of 2 miles and 4 chains on an unbroken gradient of 1 in 37.7, it is only comparable to some extent with the Dainton Bank on the former GWR between Newton Abbot and Totnes on its West of England main line. In this case, however, although both inclines on either side of the summit embody very short stretches of 1 in 36, 37 and 38, the ruling gradients are more in the region of the 1 in 50s and 60s or less.

One can of course refer to many other well known banks on several other main lines in England and Scotland, such as the famous Shap on the old LNWR, Beattock on the Caledonian, Peak Forest (now closed) and the Settle and Carlisle route, both on the Midland, Druimuachdar on the Highland, and several others in Scotland, but these are more in the nature of long hauls of several miles, mainly with gradients of between 1 in 70 and 1 in 100. The old Somerset & Dorset (another regrettable casualty) also had several severe miles either side of Masbury summit, largely of 1 in 50, whilst the former London & South Western's Ilfracombe branch, also now closed, was mainly at between 1 in 36 and 1 in 41. Very much akin to the Great Western's Dainton, but this could hardly be said to have come within the category of a main trunk route, nor perhaps can Baxenden on the Lancashire & Yorkshire between Ramsbottom and Accrington, to quote just one other example.

The Lickey Incline, however, differs in one respect in that it consists of a single ascent with no corresponding drop on the other side of the summit. With all of the others it is a question of surmounting a high ridge or range of hills as an only possible alternative to tunnelling, usually far too impracticable and costly, especially in the more mountainous regions.

Owing to the peculiar nature of the terrain in the eastern half of Worcestershire, by no means a mountainous or even hilly area (apart from the small Lickey Hill range itself, rising to about 900 feet) it so happens that any direct route between Worcester, which lies around 200 feet above sea level, and the area south of Birmingham, on a somewhat higher plateau, must ascend several hundred feet and remain roughly at that height.

To go back in history to the beginnings of the line, its origin lay in the Birmingham & Gloucester Railway, which in 1845 was amalgamated with the Bristol & Gloucester to form the Bristol & Birmingham Railway. This in turn was absorbed in 1846 by the Midland, itself the result of an amalgamation in 1844 of the Birmingham & Derby Junction, the Midland Counties, and the North Midland companies. This nucleus of the Midland Railway was eventually to become one of the four largest and most important companies right up to the 1923 grouping, the others being the London and North Western, the Great Western, and the North Eastern Railways.

The Birmingham & Gloucester Railway was incorporated by an Act of 22nd April, 1836. Three routes were originally surveyed, one of them by Brunel — who would have taken a course rather more to the east of that which was chosen; no doubt Brunel, who was of course a Great Western man, had in view some sort of eventual link-up with the GWR. This suggestion was however rejected in that it would have by-passed too many important places, such as Worcester and Cheltenham, on the way. The

Engineer whose route was finally adopted was Captain William Scarth Moorsom who submitted two alternatives, one of which lay mainly to the north-west of that which was eventually chosen.

Completion of the Route

Having obtained their Act of Incorporation the Birmingham & Gloucester promoters were eager to begin work on their new railway, and in February 1837 it was reported that construction was under way. The route chosen by Captain Moorsom presented few major difficulties, though the works included a 400 yard long tunnel through Groveley Hill near Moseley and a tunnel of similar length through the Lickey Hills at Cofton (opened-out in 1928–29). Elsewhere, there were numerous cuttings and other earthworks — the Lickey Incline itself being built mainly on embankments.

The line was substantially complete by the early months of 1840, and with the track and formation in place Captain Moorsom and his assistants busied themselves with minor works at the intermediate stations. Interestingly, one of these assistants was Herbert Spencer (1820–1903) who, in later years, was destined to become an influential writer and philosopher. Spencer was involved in a variety of work on the Bristol & Gloucester line — including the replacement of a bridge at Bromsgrove and 'friction' trials (possibly connected with adhesion on the Lickey Incline). He also criticised the longitudinal sleepers used by the Birmingham & Gloucester Railway on the grounds that they provided little lateral support.

The Birmingham & Gloucester Railway was opened from Cheltenham to Bromsgrove, at the foot of the incline, on 24th June, 1840, and completed into Birmingham, with running powers over the London & Birmingham into the latter's original terminus at Curzon Street*, on 17th December, 1840. The section between Bromsgrove and Blackwell (at the summit), that is, the Lickey Incline itself, was opened on 17th September, 1840. At the other end, the remaining link between the Midland and Bristol and the West Country was provided by the Bristol & Gloucester Railway constructed under GWR auspices to the 7 ft 0 in. gauge.

Both the GWR and the Midland were contending for this important section. Up to that time through running between Birmingham and Bristol involved a change of trains at Gloucester, and had the GWR been successful they would undoubtedly have sought to extend the broad gauge throughout to Birmingham, which would of course have included the Lickey Incline itself. Fortunately this never happened, although sometimes one wonders nowadays whether the 7 ft 0 in. gauge might not after all have been more suitable to present day requirements. However, the tale of how the Midland, by some smart work on its part, secured the B&G right under the noses of its rivals, is another story.

Bromsgrove

The Lickey Incline is, as already stated, a little over 2 miles in length. It is dead straight, and situated in pleasing, unspoiled countryside. The ascent

---

* These powers were exercised from 17th August, 1841 — until then all trains had terminated at Camp Hill station.

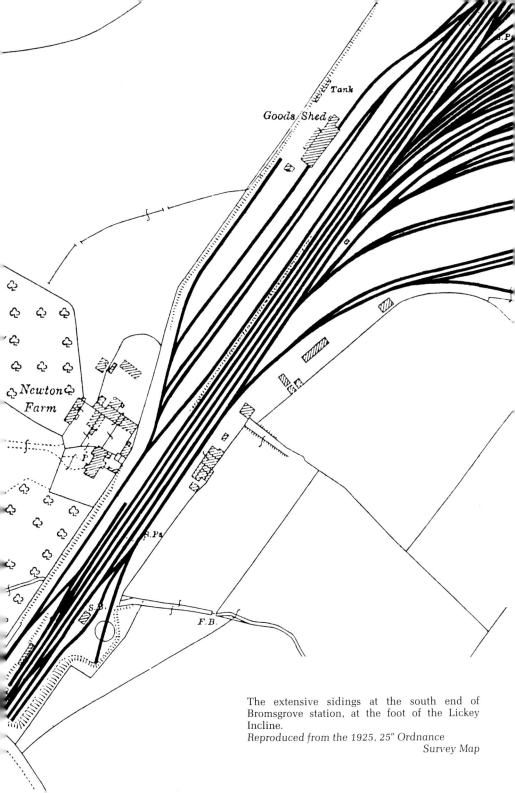

The extensive sidings at the south end of
Bromsgrove station, at the foot of the Lickey
Incline.
*Reproduced from the 1925, 25″ Ordnance
Survey Map*

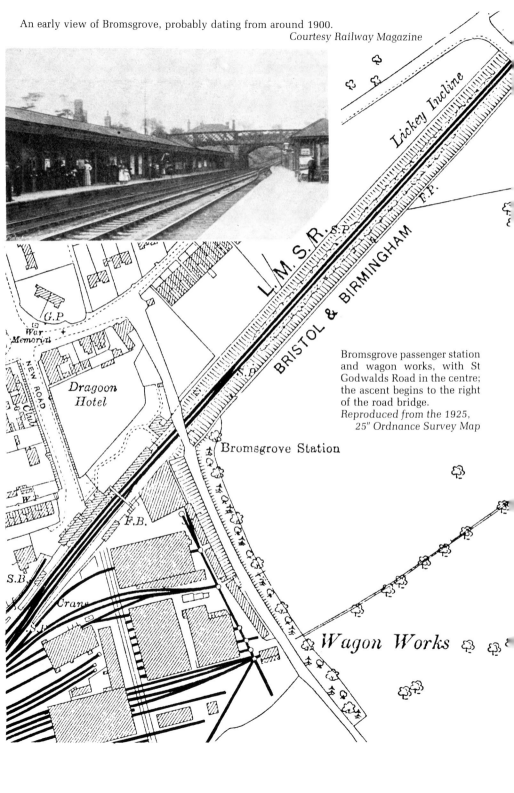

An early view of Bromsgrove, probably dating from around 1900.
Courtesy Railway Magazine

Bromsgrove passenger station and wagon works, with St Godwalds Road in the centre; the ascent begins to the right of the road bridge.
Reproduced from the 1925, 25" Ordnance Survey Map

A fine panoramic view of Bromsgrove station in the Midland era. Items of interest include the standard MR signal cabin (*left*) and the former Bristol & Gloucester Railway workshops (*right*). The Incline can be glimpsed through the distant road overbridge. *Lens of Sutton*

Looking southwards from Bromsgrove station on 11th May, 1963. Pannier tank No. 8401 awaits its next turn of duty. The photograph was taken from the rear of a northbound train. *R.M. Casserley*

Distance	STATIONS.	1 Goods A.M. ARR.	DEP.	2 Cattle and Goods A.M. ARR.	DEP.	3 Empty Wagons A.M. ARR.	DEP.	4 Passenger A.M. ARR.	DEP.	5 Express Goods A.M. ARR.	DEP.	6 Express A.M. ARR.	DEP.	7 Goods A.M. ARR.	DEP.	8 Cattle and Goods A.M. ARR.	DEP.	9 Mail P.M. ARR.	DEP.
Mls	GLOSTER -		1 0		1 0		4 30		7 0		8 40		9 30		10 0		11 15		12 40
7	Cheltenham -	1 25	1 35	1 28	1 43	4 51	4 58	7 16	7 30	9 0	9 10	9 45	9 48	10 26	10 35	11 40	11 50	12 53	12 58
10	Cleeve -	1 44		1 53		6 7	5 10	7 27	7 37	9 18		9 52		10 40		12 3	12 7	1 5	
14	Ashchurch -	1 55		5 7		5 22	5 28	7 38	7 39	9 30	9 39	9 58	10 0	10 11		5 12	20 12 25	1 14	1 16
16	Bredon -	2 0		5 14		5 31	5 38	7 41	7 45	9 41		10 3		11 12		12 31	12 35	1 19	1 20
19	Eckington -	2 9		5 21		5 47	5 52	7 53	7 54	9 50		10 7		11 23		12 45	12 60	1 28	
20	Defford -	2 12	2 20	5 27	5 35	5 55	6 0	7 57	7 58	9 53	10 15	10 10		11 27		11 32	12 53	1 0	1 31	1 32
24	Wadborough -	2 32		5 46		6 16		5 58	6 10					10 17		1 13		1 39	
25	Abbot's Wood	2 35		5 49		6 18	6 26	8 8	10 10			10 19	10 21	11 50		1 16	1 25	1 41	1 43
27	Spetchley -	2 41		6 6		6 31	6 39	8 19	20 10			10 26				1 31	1 53	1 47	1 48
31	Dunhampstead -	2 53		6 6		6 48	6 52	8 31	8 32	10 50		10 31				2 6 2	9	1 58	
33	Droitwich -	2 59		6 21		6 59	7	8 37	8 33	10 66		10 37				2 15	2 20	2 4	2 5
36	Stoke Works -	3 8		6 21		7 12	7 16	8 47	8 48	11 6		10 46		1 10	1 15	2 29	2 35	2 13	2 14
38	Bromsgrove -	3 16	3 26	6 37	6 37	7 22	7 32	8 53	5 11	11 11	11 10	52 11	7	1 22	1 32	2 45	3 10	2 18	2 30
40	Blackwell -	3 45	3 50	6 57	6 59	7 52	7 59	6 9	7 11	11 40	11 42	11	7	1 62	1 67	3 30	3 32	2 29	2 30
42	Barnt Green -	3 50		7 4		8	8 69	13 9	14 11	11 47		11 26		2 4		3 38	3 42	2 35	
46½	King's Norton -	4 8		7 16		8 19	8 29	27 9	29 11	11 59		11 20		2 8		3 55		2 42	
49	Moseley -	1 10		7 23		8 28	8 31	9 34	9 35 12	6		11 26		2 18				2 53	
51	Camp Hill -	4 22	4 33	7 37	7 33	8 42	9 40		12 11	12	12 .	11 30		2 24		4 16	4 26	2 58	
53	BIRMINGM. -	4 50		7 45		8 65		9 58		12 30		11 40		2 50		4 30		3 10	

Distance	STATIONS.	10 Goods P.M. ARR.	DEP.	11 Cattle and Goods P.M. ARR.	DEP.	12 Passenger P.M. ARR.	DEP.	13 Cattle and Goods P.M. ARR.	DEP.	14 Passenger P.M. ARR.	DEP.	15 Goods P.M. ARR.	DEP.	16 Passenger P.M. ARR.	DEP.	17 Cattle and Goods. P.M. ARR.	DEP.	18 Mail P.M. ARR.	DEP.	19 Goods P.M. ARR.	DEP.
Mls	GLOSTER -						3 21		3 30		1 32				6 15				9 0		9 15
7	Cheltenham -			1 23	1 43	3 40	3 44	3 68	4 13	48	1 60			6 33	6 31	7 21		9 13	9 15	9 36	9 50
10	Cleeve -			1 52		3 53	3 63	4 22			1 65			6 39		7 30		9 19		9 69	
14	Ashchurch -			2 4		4 4	4 14	4 34	4 39	5 3	5 4			6 41	6 52	7 42		9 27	9 31	10 12	10 17
16	Bredon -			2 10		4 14	4 14	4 45	4 50	5 12				6 47	6 68	7 48		9 35		10 23	
19	Eckington -			2 19		4 19	4 20	4 56	5 0	5 5				6 60		7 57		9 40		10 32	
20	Defford -			2 22	2 35	4 23	4 24	5 28	5 33	5 19	5 20			7 11	7 12	8 10		9 42		10 35	10 45
24	Wadborough -			2 47		4 38	4 34	5 45						7 21	7 22	8 23		9 48	9 60	11 0	
25	Abbot's Wood			2 50		4 39	4 38	5 48	5 68	5 31	5 33			7 24	7 26	8 23		9 57	10	11 0	
27	Spetchley -			2 60		4 47	4 48			5 37				7 32		8 32		9 67	10	11 6	
31	Dunhampstead -			3 8		4 59	5 0			5 46				7 44		8 43		10 8		11 18	
33	Droitwich -			3 14		5 6	5 16	5 61						7 49	7 60	8 49		10 12	10 14	11 21	
36	Stoke Works -		2 30	3 23		5 15	6	7 16						7 25	7 57	7 68	8 58		10 18		11 33	
38	Bromsgrove -	2 40	3 0	3 25	3 46	5 21	5 29	6 13	6 16	7		8 35	8 18	7	8 19	8 20	9 31	9 36	10 29	10 31	11 39	11 49
40	Blackwell -	3 20	3 25	4 6	4 7	5 34	5 35	7 6	27	7 56	6 29	8 41		8 38	8 44	9 31	9 36	10 29	12 9	12 11
42	Barnt Green -	3 31		4 16		5 40	5 41	6 48	8 17			8 63		8 38		1 56		10 40		12 17	
46½	King's Norton -	3 43		4 27		5 55	6 48	6 18	17					8 39		1 56		10 46		12 31	
49	Moseley -	4		4 32		6 0	6	18	20					8 48				10 60		12 40	
51	Camp Hill -	4 27		4 40	4 46	6 6	6 8	8 32	8 40	6 47		9 0		8 50		10 0	10 10	10 64		12 46	12 64
53	BIRMINGM. -	3 60	4	4 40	4	6 24		8 50				9 15				10 25		11 0		1 15	

A Passenger Train leaves Gloucester at 11.0 a.m.,   5 Train Shunt at Defford for   arrives at Cheltenham at 11 15 ,,   No. 6 Express Passenger Train.

8 Train Shunts at Spetchley for No. 9 Passenger Train.

No. 7 and 13 Trains runs via Worcester.   No. 16 Train Shunts at Bromsgrove for 16 Pass. Train.

13 Train Shunt for 14 Pass. Train at Eckington

Midland Railway.

GENERAL TIME-TABLES
FOR
OCTOBER, 1853.

Midland Railway working timetable for October 1853 showing only the 'up' direction train workings.

GLOUCESTER TO BIRMINGHAM.

STATIONS	SUNDAY TRAINS. 1 Empty Wagons A.M. ARR.	DEP.	2 Passenger A.M. ARR.	DEP.	3 Passenger P.M. ARR.	DEP.	4 Mail P.M. ARR.	DEP.
GLOSTER -		1 30		8 39		6 54		9 0
Cheltenham -	4 51	6 5	8 57	8 59	7 12	7 14	9 13	9 15
Cleeve -	5 7	5 10	9 6	9 7	7 21	7 22	9 19	
Ashchurch -	5 22	5 28	9 17	9 31	7 37	7 32	9 27	9 31
Bredon -	5 31	5 38	9 21	9 22	7 36	7 37	9 35	
Eckington -	5 47	5 52	9 28	9 29	7 43	7 41	9 40	
Defford -	5 55	6 0	9 32	9 33	7 47	7 48	9 42	
Wadborough -	6 12	6 16	9 42	9 46	8 0		9 48	
Abbot's Wd. -	6 18	6 25	9 46	9 48	7 69	8 0	9 48	9 50
Spetchley -	6 31	6 36	9 52	9 63	7 8	8	9 57	10 1
Dunhampstd. -	6 48	6 52	10 6	10 68	8 20	8 21	10 8	
Droitwich -	6 68	7	10 8	10 12	8 26	8 27	10 12	10 14
Stoke Works -	7 12	7 16	10 2	10 28	8 30	8 31	10 18	10 19
Bromsgrove -	7 22	7 32	10 18	10 22	8 42	8 44	10 23	10 25
Blackwell -	7 52	7 57	10 40	10 41	8 55	8 56	10 29	
Barnt Green -	8 28	6 10	10 45	10 46	9 0		10 31	
King's Nrtn. -	8 19	8 22	10 59	11	9 9	9 10	10 40	
Moseley -	8 28	8 31	11 4	11	9 19	9 20	10 45	
Camp H. Il -	8 37	8 42	11 14	11 15	9 29	9 30	10 49	
BIRMNGM. -	8 55		11 30		9 46		11 0	

commences immediately beyond the platforms at Bromsgrove, and at the summit is Blackwell station — closed to all traffic in April 1966. Even Bromsgrove, although nominally serving an important township with a population of some 10,000, is now but a shadow of its former self. Its great drawback lies in the fact that the station is inconveniently situated, being over a mile from the town centre.

At one time Bromsgrove residents enjoyed a good service of trains to and from Birmingham, but nowadays all that is left is a sporadic local service between Worcester and Barnt Green — from where connections are available to Birmingham and Lichfield. All trains run from the former up platform, that on the down side having been demolished.* There was also a through centre running road through the station, used by down expresses not calling there, and also by the descending banking engines returning from the summit to await their turn for the next 'push'.

In its heyday, Bromsgrove had exhibited a variety of interesting features. The main station building was on the up side, and this somewhat ramshackle structure incorporated at least two different periods of construction; the much smaller down side building was, in contrast, a characteristic Midland-type waiting room. The up and down platforms were linked by a lattice girder footbridge, and there was a classic MR hip-roofed signal cabin on the up side.

There was an extensive yard to the south of the station (once a scene of busy activity) and also a small running shed for the banking engine adjacent to a sizeable wagon repair works, formerly the locomotive headquarters of the Birmingham & Gloucester Railway.

At the southern end of Bromsgrove yard on the up side was a siding for the servicing of the banking engines, with a coal stage, and of course, watering facilities. Today, much of the area to the west of the railway is occupied by an oil depot. Up freight trains had a long goods loop in which they could await their turn for the ascent between the passenger services.

Leaving Bromsgrove station, northbound trains pass under St Godwalds Road, the overbridge provided here being a modern concrete structure — though in steam days there had been a traditional stone arched bridge. Entering a cutting the route starts to climb, and with houses and bungalows visible to the right, trains soon pass beneath another road overbridge carrying Finstall Road over the line. Emerging from the cutting the railway reaches a long embankment which is pierced, in two places, by small underbridges or cattle creeps; the view ahead is entirely unimpeded, and travellers in the front seats of the older type diesel multiple units are rewarded with a superb vista, extending upwards for two miles towards Blackwell summit.

Continuing north-eastwards along the dead straight, 1 in 37½ incline, northbound trains run through pastoral countryside. Still on an embankment, the route passes over two road underbridges in quick succession. The first of these takes the railway over Stratford Road, while the second is a large modern structure spanning the main A448 road; this second bridge

---

* A new down platform was due to be opened on Monday 14th May, 1990.

Bromsgrove south sidings and locomotive spur seen on 25th May, 1951. A class 3F stands at the coaling stage (*left*) while 'Big Bertha' approaches on the down line; a southbound freight is held by the South Box.   H.C. Casserley

Bromsgrove station on 1st August, 1922, with 'Big Bertha' about to assist an up passenger working towards Blackwell. Note that there were three lines through the station, the centre line being used by down trains not calling at the station. Such trains were supposed to run through at no more than 10 mph. The start of the up incline can clearly be seen in this view.   H.C. Casserley

was built in the mid-1970s when the present road replaced Stratford Road as a major traffic artery. With Caspidge Farm prominent to the right, the railway continues its relentless ascent, and having reached the half-way point between Bromsgrove and Blackwell summit, trains pass over a further underbridge, by means of which a minor road known as Pikes Pool Lane crosses from the right to the left hand side of the line.

Blackwell

Running parallel with Pikes Pool Lane, the Incline maintains its north-easterly heading. At this point the railway is cut into a great ledge, the land on the right hand side of the line being much higher than that to the left; a glance to the right reveals an expanse of exposed rock where the 19th century railway builders hacked and blasted their way through the hills.

Beyond, the route reaches a further stretch of embankment, the earth-works at this northern end of the incline being noticeably larger than those on the southern part of the route. Nearing the summit, trains pass over two more underbridges — one spanning Alcester Road and the other a minor road known as Alvechurch Lane. The actual summit is situated in a cutting, the abandoned station at Blackwell being just 6 chains beyond the stop board at the top of the incline. The relevant distances are as follows:

> Stoke Works Junction 00 miles 00 chains
> Bromsgrove Station   02 miles 13 chains
> Blackwell stop board 04 miles 21 chains
> Blackwell Station   04 miles 27 chains
> Barnt Green Station   05 miles 56 chains

Blackwell was a simple, wayside station, with slightly-staggered plat-forms and a two-siding goods yard on the up side of the line. There was an additional dead-end siding behind the down platform, and an array of goods lines to the north of the station enabled freight workings to be held clear of the main line while passenger trains (which had priority) descended the incline.

The main station building was on the up side and there was an additional waiting room on the down platform. The main building was a typical Midland design, with a substantial platform canopy; it was similar to Berkeley, Bakewell and other MR stations — suggesting that it had been planned by the Manchester architect Edward Walters (who designed several stations on the MR London extension and elsewhere). The platforms were fenced with the usual Midland-style diagonal fencing, and there was another standard MR hip-roofed signal cabin on the up side of the line.

Working Methods

In steam days all but the very lightest trains required banking assistance. Northbound express passenger trains not calling at Bromsgrove would come to a halt to the south of the station to enable the banking engine or engines to draw up to the rear before commencing the ascent. They were never

The summit, looking south from Blackwell station around 1930.   *H.C. Casserley*

Another view looking south from the up platform at Blackwell with the top of the Lickey Incline clearly visible; the date is 4th May, 1949.   *H.C. Casserley*

An earlier view of Blackwell station, and the top of the Lickey Incline.
Courtesy Railway Magazine

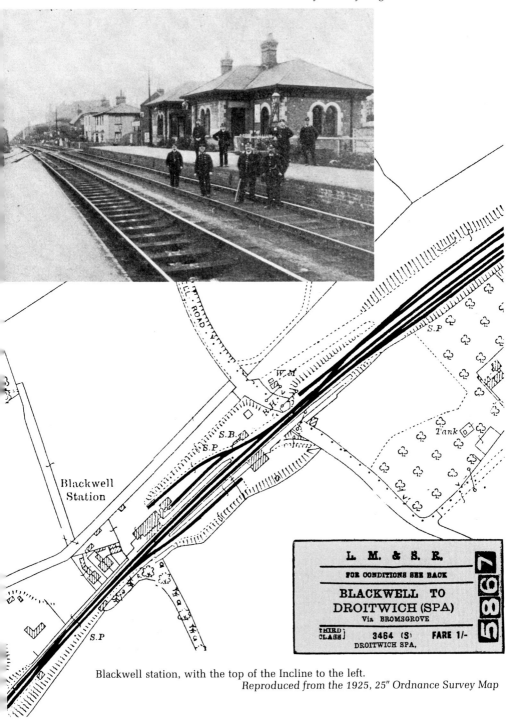

Blackwell station, with the top of the Incline to the left.
Reproduced from the 1925, 25" Ordnance Survey Map

The main station building at Blackwell was a typical Midland-style structure. This c.1960 view shows the station looking south towards Bromsgrove. (The canopy was a late addition.) *H.C. Casserley*

Ex-Midland class 4F 0−6−0 No. 3840 passes slowly through Blackwell on 12th July, 1939. *H.C. Casserley*

coupled up, either on passenger or freight trains, so there was no necessity to stop a second time at the summit at Blackwell; the banker just dropped off behind and was diverted to a siding to await an opportunity to return. Often three or four bankers would descend coupled together to avoid unnecessary line occupation, it once being the practice never to allow two trains on either line on the incline together, although in the case of the up line a slow moving train could occupy the section for too long a time — with consequent delays to following traffic, and an intermediate signal had to be installed to provide an additional block section.

The driver of the train engine, when given the all clear signal to proceed, would give a recognised call on his whistle, one long blast followed by two short ones (X-xx-xx). The initial whistle would be answered in the same code by the banking engine, the train driver responding by one short blast, answered again by the banker, upon which both would open up on full regulator to gain as much momentum as possible before the full impact of the gradient was felt by the weight of the whole train — after that it would just be one hard slog up the continuous ascent to Blackwell.

A closer look at the northern end of Bromsgrove station, this time photographed in June 1950. 'Big Bertha' stands in the down platform road. *H.C. Casserley*

No. 222, a six-coupled, Midland Railway tank locomotive as used on the Lickey Incline for banking duties in the 1860s. *Courtesy Railway Magazine*

Two of the six-coupled tank engines used for banking on the Lickey Incline by the Midland Railway in the early 1900s. *Courtesy Railway Magazine*

Midland Railway General Regulations provide a useful insight into working methods on the incline, and these regulations (which remained in force with little alteration throughout the LMS period) may be worth quoting. The 1914 MR working appendix, for example, stated that all up trains requiring assistance should be 'brought to a stand at Bromsgrove'. In general, most northbound trains required assistance, but the regulations stipulated that 'passenger trains formed of not more than equal to six vehicles' and 'mineral trains of not more than eight wagons' were allowed to ascend unassisted. Similarly, 'Goods trains of not more than ten wagons, and empty wagon trains of not more than fifteen wagons' could go up the incline 'unassisted by a bank engine' provided that the last vehicle was a brake van with a guard in charge.

These regulations were retained in the 1937 LMS Sectional Appendix, but by 1960 the limit for unassisted northbound passenger trains had been reduced to a load of four vehicles of not more than 90 tons; the limit for freight trains, meanwhile, remained unchanged until 1964 when the new loading instructions stipulated a limit of 14 wagon units.

With freight trains the driver usually left much of the work to the banker; after all, what were they there for? If one watched carefully the ascent of a loose-coupled freight train, it could usually be seen that the first few wagons had their couplings fully stretched, indicating that their load was being taken by the train engine, whilst the majority of the wagons towards the rear were buffer to buffer, obviously the effort of the banking engine. No such apportionment of the relative work on a passenger train of close coupled vehicles would of course be visible.

Once over the summit, the train would pick up speed and the bankers drop off as already described. Nowadays the picture is a very different one; diesel haulage has rendered banking assistance almost unnecessary. At Bromsgrove, the layout has been modified to allow trains to rush the bank at 80 mph and at Blackwell summit a remodelling of the vertical arc has enabled the speed restriction to be raised to 75 mph, a figure which is often achieved in practice, very different from the laborious 20 or 25 mph at the most, which was about all the trains were able to achieve in steam days.

The operation of trains descending the incline was simple enough so far as passenger or any continuous brake fitted trains were concerned, although an overall speed limit of about 25–30 mph was usually observed. Unfitted freight trains were however more of a problem. All had to be halted at Blackwell and the hand brakes on every third or fourth wagon were fastened down before the train could be allowed to proceed — and the process was of course reversed in the sidings at Bromsgrove.

The Midland Railway General Regulations again provide a wealth of operational detail in connection with descending passenger and freight trains, and some of the relevant instructions are quoted below:

3. The Brakesmen must be careful to ascertain that the brakes pinned down are in good order, and they must increase the brake power ... should they consider it necessary to do so, in consequence of the state of the weather, or from any other cause. Brakesmen need not accompany trains down the incline except when the number of Guards is not sufficient to apply the prescribed number of hand brakes.

A vintage view of Kirtley 2–4–0 No. 160 as it climbs the bank (with a tank engine banking), photographed probably around 1900. *H.C. Casserley*

Class 3 4–4–0 No. 771 ascends towards Blackwell while 'Big Bertha' assists at the rear. *E.R. Morten*

4. Guards must apply the ordinary hand brakes when descending the Incline whether the vehicles in which they are travelling are fitted with a Continuous brake in use from the engine or not.

5. Passenger trains must not descend the Incline in less than five minutes, or at a greater speed than twenty-seven miles per hour, and Goods trains in less than twelve minutes, or at a greater speed than eleven miles per hour.

6. Down Passenger trains not booked to stop at Bromsgrove must run on the down middle line between the platforms, and Drivers must, after satisfying themselves that their brakes are in good working order, reduce the speed of their trains so as to pass over the down middle line at a speed not exceeding 10 MILES PER HOUR.

All Down Passenger trains booked to stop at Bromsgrove for traffic purposes must be brought to a stand at the down platform.

All Down Goods and Mineral trains must be brought to a stand between the Passenger Station and the South Box with the rear vehicle clear of the connection between the down platform line and the down passenger line at the Bristol end of the Station . . . On arrival at Bromsgrove, any brakes that may have been applied, must be released, unless it is necessary for them to remain on for any purpose. Drivers must not proceed, after their trains have been brought to a stand, until they have obtained the usual signal from the Guard to do so.

On a footnote, it might be added that as regards the overall flow of freight traffic, the general balance was rather in favour of the working of the Incline, in that down trains would often consist of weighty loads of coal from the Midlands, uncompensated by any corresponding heavy tonnage in the reverse direction to be hauled up the bank, which must certainly have been of some operational advantage.

The ascent of a passenger train would usually take about seven minutes, but a freight often very much more, and as many as three banking engines would sometimes be necessary. At normal weekday periods there would usually be six engines available, possibly only five if one of them was the 0–10–0 'Big Bertha', which appeared on the scene in 1920, otherwise the entire work had to be performed by 0–6–0T engines supplemented by an occasional 0–6–0 tender locomotive.

Exactly what the economics of having one large engine and several small ones were has never been very clear. Possibly on a Sunday or at times when the traffic was very light, the one large engine would be found sufficient, with considerable economies in cost, but why it was never considered worth while having two of them cannot be easily explained. The practice even persisted after the regrettable demise in 1956 of the 0–10–0 by the substitution of one, and again one only, of the BR standard class '9' 2–10–0s.

There was a short period around 1949 when there were in fact two large engines on the job together, the second being the LNER Gresley 2–8–8–2 Garratt; this locomotive had been made redundant by the electrification of the Worsborough Incline, for which it had been built, but its stay at Lickey was short lived. A fuller history of the engines which have banked on the Incline over the years will be described later. This however seems an appropriate point at which to refer to Dr Ransome Wallis's intriguing

Class 3F 0−6−0 No. 43667 approaches Blackwell with a northbound working on 4th May, 1949.   H.C. Casserley

Kirtley double-framed class 1 0−6−0 No. 2825 at Blackwell with an up freight; these engines were perhaps the most commonly used goods locomotives in pre-grouping days.   LGRP (Leslie Good Collection)

experience, told in an article in *Trains Illustrated* for August 1950, from which I take the liberty of quoting extracts with his kind authority. On this memorable, and what must surely be unique, occasion he found an up freight train consisting of 42 loaded wagons in Bromsgrove yard, hauled, most unusually for this line, by LMS 2–6–6–2 Garratt No. 47972. Now to quote verbatim from Dr Ransome Wallis's racy account:

'What a picture if THAT is banked by the LNE Garratt,' I said to Don;* and sure enough, 69999 moved on to its tail. With 'crows' from the whistles of the two Garratts and with clouds of black smoke pouring from their chimneys, the two great engines set off up the bank with their 'forty two of freight' — ten cylinders working hard. Don and I ran to our car, and were soon going flat out for our spot on the lineside, where we should be able to get pictures of both engines as they went by. But we need not have hurried, for the Garratts were labouring slowly and sadly and ever more slowly, until with a deep groaning sigh, the two great engines gave it up altogether, and with clouds of smoke rolling from their chimneys, came to a very full stop about a hundred yards from where we were waiting. As if to show her superiority over her LNE sister, 47972 started blowing off, but it got her nowhere, and for 38 minutes the train was well and truly stalled. Then came signs of activity from the Bromsgrove end and soon after, more 'crows' on the whistles indicated that help had arrived. And what help! For our forty-two wagons of freight finally went up the bank with LMS Garratt No. 47972 in front, LNER Garratt No. 69999 as first banker and Midland 0–10–0 No., 58100 as second banker. Fourteen cylinders for forty-two wagons! What a sight!

A fitting climax to a day packed with interest and variety. I later recounted the incident to an LMS shed foreman. 'Aye,' he said, 'I can well believe it.' Later still, I told my story to an Eastern Region shed foreman. 'Rotten shame' he said, (in much more picturesque language, mind you!) 'Those Midland men are not trying to work our Garratt properly, and I have heard that they are trying to *sabotage* it.' Old loyalties die hard! What a shame it is that they have to die at all!

In direct contrast to Dr Ransome Wallis's experience, I would like to relate a couple of my own, of trains ascending without the services of a banker at all. The first was in 1926, and the engine a most unlikely type for such an occurrence, nothing other than the original Johnson single No. 600. I must hasten to add, however, that it spent its declining years hauling the directors' saloon around the system, so that the spectacle of its sedately hauling its load of some 30 tons or so up the incline was not very surprising after all.

The second occasion was as amusing in its way as the two Garratts plus the 0–10–0 just recounted, in a completely opposite context. Compound No. 41090 arrived at Bromsgrove station one day in April 1958 with a local to Birmingham consisting of three non-corridor coaches. A banker in the shape of GWR pannier tank No. 8404 was indeed provided, but for some reason the driver decided, perhaps in a fit of whimsical humour, that he did not require any assistance. Maybe he was one of the diminishing number of protagonists of these engines, then falling into disrepute owing to lack of maintenance, in respect of which their special peculiarities were particularly unsuited. Possibly he was even an old time dedicated Midland man, who would scorn any help from 'one of those Western interlopers'.

* (Don Kelk, his companion on the trip.)

Anyway, he decided to show just what he could do and set off with such vigour, at full blast, obviously working the engine to its maximum capacity by the use of high pressure steam in all three cylinders, as was possible with these engines, that the banker was unable to keep up with him. The spectacle of the pannier tank trying to catch up with the train it was supposed to be assisting was laughable in the extreme and not easily forgotten. I estimated that No. 41090 succeeded in maintaining a steady 35 mph or so all the way up, unusual in steam days even with a light load.

I must mention a third occasion, also in 1958, late one summer evening waiting on Blackwell station for the last train down to Bromsgrove, where I was staying the night. There was the sound of a train in the distance laboriously making the ascent proceeding at less than 10 mph. I could hear only one engine, and thought it was another unbanked train, but this eventually turned out not to be the case, although from the sound of it the train engine seemed to be doing all the work. When it finally arrived after an interval of about 15 minutes it turned out to be a local freight train consisting of about 12 wagons hauled by Johnson class '3' 0–6–0 No. 43762 running tender first. The unenthusiastic banker turned out to be 0–6–0 pannier No. 8404 again. Probably the working regulations forbade the ascent of an unbraked train without an engine at the rear, as in the case of a breakaway the guard's van might be unable to hold the wagons. The unsuperheated engine with the old fashioned short travel slide valve however made a magnificent sound echoing from the small hills of the surrounding countryside, and is one which perhaps lingers most in my memory amongst my many very memorable personal recollections of the incline.

Some of these unforgettable sounds have fortunately been preserved for all time on gramophone records, at first produced privately by Peter Handford of Princes Risborough, under the title of Transacord, but now issued under the Argo label of the Decca company. Most are of the modern 12-inch long-playing variety, some in stereo, but there were originally two 10-inch 78 rpms, on which could be heard the throaty exhaust of 'Big Bertha's' four cylinders, and recorded about 1954. Although not currently available, it is to be hoped that this valuable historic recording may sometime be reissued in 33 rpm format.

It was unfortunate that old No. 2290 (or 58100, to quote its BR number) went before the preservation movement got under way; had it lasted a little longer it would surely have qualified as a worthy candidate for honourable retirement. It spent its whole working life of 36 years pounding its way up the bank. Its recorded mileage in 1955, a year before its withdrawal, was 810,398, so that a final total must have been well short of the million mark, but still an impressive achievement, bearing in mind that it was almost entirely made up of short runs of 2½ miles. Regrettably all that we have left is its distinctive and unique sound, which can still be enjoyed by those of us fortunate enough to possess the early records.

Another classic photograph of an up train at Blackwell summit, the locomotive being class 2 No. 505. The year is 1939.   *E.R. Morten*

In 1958 the Western Region sent large tank engines to Bromsgrove for use on the Incline, the engines concerned being '72XX' 2–8–2T No. 7235 (allocated to Worcester) and '52XX' 2–8–0 No. 5226 (initially allocated to Hereford). The 2–8–2T was unsuitable because its 9 ft wide cylinder block fouled Bromsgrove platform. However, No. 5226 remained for several months, and was officially transferred to Bromsgrove in November 1959; this 1959 view shows the ex-GWR 2–8–0T dropping away from the rear of a train at Blackwell.   *H.C. Casserley*

Double-headed class 2P 4−4−0s speeding through Bromsgrove South working the York to Bristol express service in the summer of 1929.   *H.C. Casserley*

A loose-coupled freight working pauses at the top of the Incline while additional brakes are pinned down.   *H.C. Casserley*

Part Two

Lickey Bankers and Other Locomotives

Having sketched-in something of the early history and development of the Lickey Incline it would now be appropriate to examine some of the engines that have worked over the route.The first engines to be discussed will be the famous Norris singles which were, as a matter of interest, among the very few American engines to work in England.

The Norris Singles

The earliest engines to be employed as 'Lickey Bankers' were five 4−2−0s designed by and obtained from William Norris of Philadelphia, and delivered to the Birmingham & Gloucester Railway, three between May and December 1840 and the other two in May 1842. The price of these loco-motives was said to have been 'between £1,500 and £1,600 each, including the import duty at 20 per cent'. They were known as Norris Class A (Extra) and had 4 ft driving wheels, 2 ft 6 in. carrying wheels and 12 in. × 20 in. inside cylinders. Typical American features included the use of bar frames and the Bury-type rounded firebox. The weight of these engines was said by David Joy to have been 'about eight' tons; 'the little thing could pull', he conceded, 'but she was odd, plenty of cast iron in her, even the crosshead pins were cast iron'.

Other Norris type 4−2−0s, known as Class A, with 11½ in. cylinders, were supplied by William Norris (3), Benjamin Hick of Bolton (3), and Nasmyth Gaskell & Co., of Patricroft (6), between 1839 and 1841. Others known as Class B with 10½ in. cylinders were supplied by William Norris (7) in 1839 and 1840, or acquired from Thomas Banks of Manchester in 1840 (2).

The total number of Norris type 4−2−0s acquired by the Birmingham & Gloucester was thus 26 (5 Class A Extra, 12 Class A and 9 Class B) but only the five Class A Extra types were used as banking engines. The others were responsible for all general traffic, both passenger and goods, over the B&G during its first years. Birmingham & Gloucester engines originally carried names only, but at some date between May 1842 and November 1844 they were given numbers as well.

The question might well be asked as to why such a type as the 4−2−0 should have been chosen at all, particularly for banking duties; although at that period it would not have been quite so curious for ordinary service, the 2−2−2 was more generally preferred on most railways. The choice was apparently that of Captain W.S. Moorsom, who was the civil engineer in charge of the construction of the Birmingham & Gloucester Railway and found himself saddled also with the mechanical side of things, including of course the supply of locomotives for the line. Little experience had yet been had in this country of working a gradient as steep as 1 in 37, or anything like it, and Captain Moorsom seems to have been impressed by the performance of an early design of Norris engine, the *George Washington*, which had been

tried out on a 1 in 14 gradient worked mainly by a cable on the Portsmouth &
Roanoke Railway in America, to be followed in the same year by the very
similar engine *Washington County Farmer*, which was in effect the prototype of the four standard designs of Norris 4–2–0s to be built in large
numbers and exported to many countries abroad.

By the end of 1840, no less than 135 had been built, mostly for general
duties, although their suitability for hill climbing seems to have been
demonstrated sufficiently to Captain Moorsom for him to decide to adopt
the type for the Birmingham & Gloucester in March 1839.

Writing in the 1890s, W.J. Gordon was in no doubt that the decision to
employ the Norris engines was Captain Moorsom's. The Lickey was, he said:

> The steepest gradient on a main line in this island. It rises 1 in 37 for two miles;
> and yet, unlike all other steep inclines on the older roads, it has always been
> worked by locomotives. Brunel and George Stephenson had said no locomotives
> could get up it; and in days when it was thought inevitable that there should be
> stationary engines to drag the trains up out of Euston and Liverpool, it was not a
> little startling to find an engineer stoutly declaring that up the Lickey he would
> send his train, and ropes he would have none ... All the same, Brunel and
> Stephenson were correct within a certain limitation. By 'no engine' they meant 'no
> existing English engine'. But Captain Moorsom had been in America, where he had
> seen engines go up even sharper gradients, and it was with American bogie
> engines having driving wheels of only four feet that he drew his first trains up the
> Lickey. These engines have long been superseded, the last of them used to be on
> the Tewkesbury branch — which was at first worked by horses — but they are
> worth remembrance. They were not the first bogies, for the bogie was invented on
> this side of the Atlantic, and there were bogie engines on the Dundee and Newtyle
> line as early as 1833.

The Birmingham & Gloucester Railway and the Bristol & Gloucester
Railway amalgamated as from 14th January, 1845, the new company being

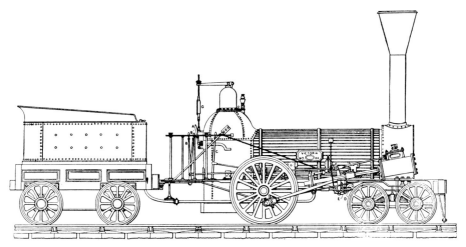

A Class B Norris engine No. 6 *Victoria*, one of the original 4–2–0s used on the
Birmingham & Gloucester Railway, although not actually one of the five Class A
engines allocated specifically to banking duties.

known as the Bristol & Birmingham Railway, and this in turn was taken over by the Midland Railway on 3rd August, 1846. The locomotive stock was renumbered into the Midland list in February 1847.

The five Class A Extra bankers became Midland Nos. 217–275, and those remaining at June 1852 were further renumbered. The last two were withdrawn in June 1856. The first three were rebuilt as 4–2–0 saddle tanks in 1842. The date of rebuilding of the last two is not known and may have been in 1842 shortly after delivery, or at some later date. These five are listed in the 1849 Midland list as 4–2–0 passenger engines with 12 in. × 20 in. cylinders and 5 ft 0 in. driving wheels and they are the only Norris type engines in this list. Details of the five engines are as follows:

Name	Later Numbered	Delivered	Converted to ST	First MR No. 2/1847	Renumbered 6/1852	Disposal
Philadelphia	13	5/1840	3/1842	271	113	Broken up 6/1856
Boston	14	8/1840	By 8/1842	272	114	Broken up 6/1856
Gwynn	21	12/1840	,,	273	(115) allotted	Sold 5/1852 to a Mr Knox for £250
Niagara	31	5/1842	,,	274		Sold 5/1851 to a Mr C.H. Smith (a coal owner in the Swansea area) for £200
New York	32	,,	,,	275	104	Sold 4/1855 to a Mr John Wood of Derby for £200

An Experimental 0–2–2T

This engine is mentioned several times in the minutes of the Birmingham & Gloucester Railway, but it was never their property.

It appears to have been built in 1836 for a Mr S.A. Goddard. It had 6 ft 2½ in. driving wheels, 3 ft 0 in. trailing carrying wheels, and outside cylinders 11¼ in. × 20 in., and was double-framed and with inside bearings. In January 1838 it was tried on the London & Birmingham Railway as a ballast engine, and in March 1838 it was advertised for sale under the name Victoria.

On 3rd November, 1840 the Birmingham & Gloucester Railway Directors gave their agreement to Mr Goddard trying it for a month on their line 'with the trains', by which time it had been renamed Surprise. On 10th November its boiler burst through a weakness in the plates, killing the driver, Thomas Scaife; Fireman Joseph Rutherford, who was also on the footplate, died the next day from his injuries.

This tragedy cast a dark cloud over the experimental 0–2–2T and when, on 25th January, 1842, Mr Goddard again offered to try his engine — by then renamed *Eclipse* — on the Bromsgrove incline, the offer was declined.

On 26th January, 1844 it was ordered that Mr Goddard's former engine, now in the hands of the Birmingham Banking Company, be allowed a trial on the line 'when they have made their own repairs and alterations thereto', but it would appear that nothing came of this. Six years later, in 1850, it was standing at Camp Hill Station, Birmingham, and in February 1852 *Eclipse* was advertised for sale, still standing at Camp Hill Station.

Between then and 1857 it was sold to a coal owner near Swansea, and in 1857 it was in the workshops of the Swansea Vale Railway in pieces. A Mr T.W. Turner then utilised its boiler, lengthened, and with an increased number of tubes and with her big dome, in a new small wheeled 0–6–0 which he built for heavy mineral trains using sharply curved tracks. Its subsequent history seems to be unknown.

Reverting briefly to the fatal explosion at Bromsgrove station on 10th November, 1840, it is interesting to recall that the remains of driver Scaife and fireman Rutherford were interred in Bromsgrove churchyard and commemorated by a pair of prominent memorial stones that have survived to this day. The fact that both embody finely executed carvings of a Norris engine has often given rise to the erroneous impression that it was one of these engines which exploded, which of course it was not. A likely explanation is that the stonemason was given a drawing of a Norris to work from, probably the only suitable picture locally available, and which he

The famous tombstones in Bromsgrove churchyard commemorating the tragic deaths of Thomas Scaife and Joseph Rutherford as a result of a boiler explosion at the station on 10th November, 1840.   *Oakwood Collection*

The tombstones display appropriate poems which are worth quoting:

My engine now is cold and still,
No water doth my boiler fill:
My coke affords its flame no more,
My days of usefulness are o'er.
My wheels deny their noted speed
No more my guiding hands they heed.
My whistle, too, has lost its tone,
Its shrill and thrilling sounds are gone,
My valves are now thrown open wide,
My flanges all refuse to guide.
My clacks, also, though once so strong,
Refuse to aid the busy throng.
No more I feel each urging breath,
My steam is now condensed in death.
Life's railway's o'er, each station's past,
In death I'm stopped and rest at last.
Farewell dear friends, and cease to weep
In Christ I'm SAFE, in Him I sleep.

The verses continue on fireman Rutherford's tombstone, which was erected by his widow; the first six lines being as follows:

Oh Reader stay and cast an eye,
Upon this grave wherein I lie.
For cruel death has challenged me,
And soon alas will call on thee:
Repent in time, make no delay,
For Christ will call you all away.

The deceased enginemen are described as 'engineers' to the Birmingham and Gloucester Railway, and the inscription of Thomas Scaife's headstone records that the poem was 'composed by an unknown friend'.

McConnell's Great Britain

The next engine to be considered is an 0–6–0T designed by James F. McConnell, the Superintendent of Workshops, and built at the Bromsgrove works of the Birmingham & Gloucester Railway specifically for 'assisting the trains on the Lickey'. It had 18 in. × 26 in. outside cylinders and 3 ft 10 in. coupled wheels, and weighed 30 tons. It was at that date the most powerful locomotive in the country. The boiler was of oval section, the vertical diameter being 3 ft 10 in. and the horizontal 3 ft 9 in.

Completed in June 1845, it was numbered 38 and named *Great Britain*; the engine was numbered 276 by the MR and renumbered 105 in June 1852. It was rebuilt at Derby in January 1853 as a 0–6–0WT banker with 16 in. × 24 in. inside cylinders, retaining its 3 ft 10 in. coupled wheels and oval boiler, and was renumbered 300. It was further renumbered 221 in June 1855, and was finally withdrawn from service in October 1861, being broken up in July 1862.

0–6–0 and 0–6–0T Bankers

In February 1847 instructions were given that 'two of the engines already ordered from Robt Stephenson & Co. be altered to suit the Lickey Incline'. These two were double framed 0–6–0s with 4 ft 6 in. driving wheels and 17 in. × 24 in. cylinders below the leading axle and they had special low tenders — they were not 'long boilered'. Details are:

No. as built	Date	Makers No.	Renumbered	Broken up
200	12/1847	601	215 1/1851	7/1858
201	2/1848	602	216 1/1851	9/1859

Four outside framed 0–6–0WTs with 4 ft 2 in. driving wheels and 16½ in. × 24 in. cylinders were built new in 1860–63 as Lickey bankers as under:

No. as built	Date	Renumbered		Rebuilt	Withdrawn
320	12/1860	220	5/66	As 0–6–0 with	
		220A	9/79	5 ft 2½ in. wheels and	11/1899
				16 in. × 24 in. cylinders	
				12/1883 retaining	
				No. 220A	

No. as built	Date	Renumbered		Further Renumbered	Withdrawn
222	12/1860	222A	3/90		2/1894
223	12/1862	223A	1/90	1604, 5/1907; LMS 1607/1923	7/1928
221	12/1863	221A	10/79	1431, 12/87; 1431A, 3/1890	5/1901

Ten miscellaneous 0–6–0s were rebuilt as 0–6–0WTs at dates between 1862 and 1875 and used as Lickey bankers, and in three cases finally reverted to 0–6–0 tender engines as detailed below:

146   Derby 12/1851. Rebuilt as 0–6–0WT with 4 ft 2 in. wheels and 16 in. × 24 in. cylinders 8/1862 and renumbered 318. Withdrawn 3/1867 as No. 217.

206   Robert Stephenson 607 3/1848. Renumbered 201 1/1851, Rebuilt as 0–6–0WT with 4 ft 9 in. wheels, 15 in. × 24 in. cylinders 12/1862 (201). Withdrawn 3/1870 as No. 1038.

221   Originally 'Crampton' 2 × 2–2–0 Kitson 130 of 9/1848 and numbered MR 101. Reconstructed by Kitson as 0–6–0 1849/50 and renumbered 221. Renumbered 230 by 9/1851 and 218 in 6/1855. Rebuilt as 0–6–0WT, 4 ft 8 in. wheels. 16½ in. × 24 in. cylinders 12/1862 (218). Withdrawn 11/1873 as No. 2016.

222   Ditto Kitson 131 of 10/1848 and numbered MR 102. Ditto and renumbered 222. Renumbered 231 by 9/1851 and 219 in 6/1855. Rebuilt as 0–6–0WT as above 12/1862 (219). Rebuilt again as 0–6–0WT 4 ft 2 in. wheels and 17 in. × 24 in. cylinders 11/1875 and renumbered 200. Withdrawn 7/1921 as No. 1600.

175   Derby 6/1857, Rebuilt at 0–6–0WT, 4 ft 2 in. wheels, 16½ in. × 24 in. cylinders 3/1867 and renumbered 215. Renumbered 2038 3/1873. Rebuilt again as 0–6–0WT 6/1879 (2038). Withdrawn 2/1906 as No. 2038A.

172   Derby 6/1857. Rebuilt as 0–6–0WT with 5 ft 2 in. wheels and 16 in. × 24 in.
       cylinders 3/1867 and renumbered 213. Renumbered 213A 11/1875. Rebuilt
       as 0–6–0 5 ft 2 in. wheels and 17 in. × 24 in. cylinders 10/1879 (213).
       Withdrawn 9/1899 as No. 213A.

179   Derby 9/1860. Rebuilt as 0–6–0WT, 5 ft 2 in. wheels, 16½ in. × 24 in.
       cylinders, 11/1867 and renumbered 214. Renumbered 214A 11/1875.
       Rebuilt as 0–6–0, 5 ft 2 in. wheels and 17 in. × 24 in. cylinders 11/1881
       (214A). Withdrawn 2/1897 as No. 322.

216   Derby 12/1859. Rebuilt as 0–6–0WT with 5 ft 2 in. wheels and
       16½ in. × 24 in. cylinders 12/1867. Renumbered 217A 11/1875. Rebuilt as
       0–6–0, 5 ft 2 in. wheels, 17 in. × 24 in. cylinders 8/1881 (217A). Withdrawn
       3/1905 as No. 332.

215   Kitson 183 of 8/1848. Renumbered 224 1/1851. Rebuilt 6/1857*. Taken out
       of service 1/1875 as 2034 for rebuilding as WT. Rebuilt as 0–6–0WT with
       4 ft 2 in. wheels and 16½ in. × 24 in. cylinders, 6/1875 and renumbered
       1092. Withdrawn 8/1898 as No. 1092A.

216   Kitson 185 of 10/1848. Renumbered 225 1/1851. Rebuilt 12/1857.*
       Taken out of service 1/1875 as 2035 for rebuilding as WT. Rebuilt as
       0–6–0WT 4 ft 2 in. wheels, 16½ in. × 24 in. cylinders 6/1875 and re-
       numbered 1094. Withdrawn 3/1902 as No. 1094A.

---

* Note: Other sources give these 1857 rebuilds as to 0–6–0WT with 4 ft 6 in.
  wheels and 17 in. × 24 in. cylinders. This is a probability as at this date
  there would be only three bankers as such available – 221 GREAT BRITAIN
  and 215/216 (the two 'altered' 0–6–0s) — pending the arrival of the two
  new tanks built in 1860.

An early engine built by Kirtley in December 1862; one of four specifically built for
banking on the Lickey Incline.   *Author's Collection*

A down train runs into Bromsgrove behind class 1 2–4–0 No. 174 and class 2 4–4–0 No. 507. This fine print is dated 1st August, 1922.

H.C. Casserley

A typical daily scene as class 2 4–4–0 No. 525 climbs the Incline with a northbound express passenger train; bankers assist at the rear.   *LCGB (Ken Nunn Collection)*

A double-headed passenger working pounds up the Incline behind 2–4–0 and 4–4–0 locomotives, while a banking engine provides extra help at the rear.
LCGB (Ken Nunn Collection)

The relief 'Devonian' express nears Bromsgrove station on 26th March, 1932. This photograph was taken from the Finstall Road bridge, the up line being on the left.

E.R. Morten

Class 3 0–6–0 No. 3678 climbs the Incline with a heavy train on a mixed freight working.

Real Photographs

A classic scene on the Lickey Incline as Johnson 4–2–2 No. 614 pilots a class 2 4–4–0 up the Incline towards Blackwell.   H.C. Casserley

'Big Bertha' assists a northbound freight working on the 1 in 37 Incline. As a general rule all bankers worked chimney first on the ascent, though the LNER Garrett usually worked bunker-first; note the large electric headlight which was useful during night working.   E.R. Morten

Midland Railway class 2 4−4−0 No. 405 storms up the Incline during the MR period. The metal plates in front of the leading bogie were supposed to protect engines from excessive spray when double-headed trains took water from water troughs.

Real Photographs

Around 60 years later, class 9F 2−10−0 No. 92139 reaches the summit with an up train. Flat-bottomed rail has replaced the chaired variety, but otherwise the scene is little-altered.

Lens of Sutton

A shed list drawn up at June 1892 shows that the following Johnson 0–6–0Ts were shedded at Bromsgrove: 210, 211, 212, 215, 216 (1720–1724 in the renumbering of 1907). These probably went there when new in 1883 and it is likely that they remained until replaced by the later series of 1902. No. 1720 still carried a shed 4 plate (Worcester — the parent shed) in 1924.

An official shed list at 30th April, 1914 shows Johnson 0–6–0Ts Nos. 1932–38 as shed 4, and these were sub-shedded at Bromsgrove for Lickey Incline banking duties. They probably went there when new in 1902. (They were built as Nos. 2753–2759, becoming Nos. 1932–38 under the 1907 renumbering scheme.) By 1917 Bromsgrove had exchanged No. 1932 with Brecon for No. 1955 and by April 1924 the latter had been transferred to shed 28 (Leeds), Bromsgrove received in exchange No. 1939 from shed 29 (Bradford), possibly sub-shedded at Keighley and No. 1954 from shed 21 (Manchester). In 1922, No. 1947, complete with shed 16 plates (Kentish Town) was on loan to Bromsgrove, but it was back at Cricklewood by April 1924.

In 1914 there were twelve class '1' double framed and eight single framed class '2' or '3' 0–6–0s at shed 4, and it is possible that some of these tender engines might have been utilised on banking duties in assisting the 0–6–0Ts should necessity have arisen. Kirtley 0–6–0 No. 2630 certainly seems to have been more or less permanently attached to Bromsgrove between 1916 and 1920.

The Johnson 0–6–0Ts of the '1900' class had a long reign on the Lickey Incline. During the first half of the 1920s they acquired Belpaire fireboxes, with Ramsbottom safety valves, losing the distinctive Johnson spring balance salters on the dome. As such they became the prototype of the standard LMS 0–6–0Ts, built in large numbers after 1924 and usually known as 'Jinties'; examples of this modified version gradually replaced the original Johnsons. The latter were however incorporated with the whole series by being renumbered in sequence from 7200 to 7259, whilst the standard 'Jinties' eventually ran from 7260 to 7681 (later to become BR Nos. 47260 to 47681).

Of the original Johnsons Nos. 7234 to 7239 were still there in July 1939, some of them having had an almost continuous reign of nearly 40 years. By that time they had been joined by Nos. 7425 and 7443 of the later series, both then on loan from Saltley. No. 7425 was to become a permanent resident of Bromsgrove, where it remained until 1956 (as 47425), after which it was sent away to the L&YR area.

By the 1950s the original Midland locomotives had gone away and had been replaced by Fowler '3F' 0–6–0Ts Nos. 47276, 47301, 47305, 47308, 47502 and 47576, which were the most continuous residents until 1958, although others appeared from time to time. Of special interest amongst these was No. 47313, which was originally a Somerset & Dorset engine, and was on loan to Bromsgrove in April 1957. This engine was to be of particular interest in that it was destined to be the last S&DJR locomotive to remain in ordinary service at the time of its eventual withdrawal in 1967.

It will be convenient at this time to mention that Bromsgrove was originally a sub-shed of Worcester (MR shed code 4 in pregrouping days), but under the LMS regime Bromsgrove acquired its own identity as 21C, sub-shed to Saltley Birmingham (which was 21A).

In February 1958 the whole of the line to Bristol south-west of Barnt Green became part of the Western Region, as a consequence of which Bromsgrove shed was coded 85F, as a sub-shed of Worcester (85A), but by 1962 this had been altered to 85D. A year or two later it was no longer a shed in its own right and had become what is known as a stabling point for two or three diesels based at other depots.

In accordance with this regional adjustment it was decided that the LMS 0−6−0 tank locomotives should be replaced by Swindon types, and accordingly seven 0−6−0PTs of the '94XX' class, Nos. 8400 to 8406, became permanent bankers at Bromsgrove, although as late as 1961 Nos. 47276 and 47308 were also still there, carrying 85D shedplates. Other '94XX' 0−6−0PTs used on the incline during the early 1960s included Nos. 8409, 9401, 9430 and 9493. Another resident of Bromsgrove shed during this period was class '3' 0−6−0 No. 43762, which was used on local goods trips and survived there to carry 85F plates until 1961.

Fowler's 'Big Bertha' 0−10−0

To go back somewhat in time, undoubtedly the most historic banking locomotive on the Lickey Incline, and the only one apart from McConnell's 1845 engine to be designed and built specifically for this purpose, was Sir Henry Fowler's 4 cylinder 0−10−0, which first saw the light of day in January 1920. It caused something of a sensation at the time, as only the scantiest details had been allowed to leak out from Derby as to its nature, in fact nothing more than a vague statement that 'a large banking engine is on order for the Lickey Incline'. By Midland standards in particular it was a revolutionary machine, far larger than anything that railway had previously, (not even an eight-coupled engine of any sort) but this one went the whole hog by emerging as a 'decapod' — at that time the only ten-coupled engine in the country (since that abortive experiment by the Great Eastern way back in 1902).

So far as a Lickey banker was concerned it also broke new ground by virtue of its being a tender engine, since the weight of an equivalent tank locomotive would have been too great. As it was, it was possible to limit the individual axle load to 15.5 tons. Its four cylinders 16¾in. × 28in., were steeply inclined at one in seven, and the employment of Walschaert's valve gear was almost unique on the Midland, although this had been used by Deeley on some small 0−4−0T dock shunters which first appeared in 1907. The driving wheels were 4ft 7½in. in diameter and at a working pressure of 180 lb. it developed a tractive effort of 43,315 lb. The weight of the engine in working order was 73.67 tons.

Soon after it was put into traffic it was fitted with an electric headlight to facilitate drawing up gently on to the rear of a train in darkness, and in later years the top part of the tender cowling was cut away to give better rear visibility. Incidentally it had two boilers, one being kept spare at Derby so

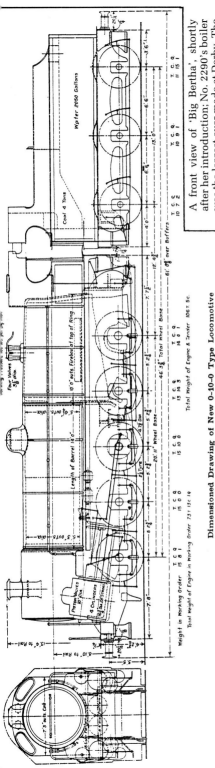

Dimensioned Drawing of New 0-10-0 Type Locomotive

Water 2050 Gallons

Coal 4 Tons

Four Valves 3½ dia.

10'0 outs Firebox at top of Ring

Length of Barrel 14'0"

5'4½ outs. dia.

4'7¾ Dia

20'11 Wheel Base

46 3¾ Total Wheel Base

5'3 outs dia.

Piston Valves 10" DIA

4 Cylinders
16¾ Dia. 28 Stroke

7'8

13'4 to Rail

8'10" to Rail

5'5

7'5 outs Cab

61 0⅛ over Buffers

Weight in Working Order
T.C.Q T.C.Q T.C.Q T.C.Q T.C.Q
15 8 1 15 0 0 15 0 0 14 0 0 13 14 3

Total Weight of Engine in Working Order 73.1.13c 1q

Total Weight of Engine & Tender 106.7.5c

T.C.Q T.C.Q T.C.Q
11 15 1 10 9 1 10 7 2

Total Weight of Engine 0-10-0 Type Locomotive

3.6.1

6.6"   15.0"   6.6"   4.0"

A front view of 'Big Bertha', shortly after her introduction: No. 2290's boiler was the largest ever made at Derby. The prominent headlamp was later fitted to class 9F 2–10–0 No. 92079.
LCGB (Ken Nunn Collection)

The author captures 'Big Bertha', No. 2290 during a test steaming just days after completion at Derby works, on 1st January, 1920.
H.C. Casserley

An impressive view of 'Big Bertha' shortly after her introduction in the 1920s. The location is probably near Blackwell station.   *H.C. Casserley*

Another impressive photograph of 'Big Bertha' waiting on the down main line at Blackwell in the summer of 1939. The engine has just banked an up working and she is now awaiting for a clear road back to Bromsgrove.   *E.R. Morten*

that when it went into shops for repairs the boiler could be exchanged, so reducing very considerably the amount of time spent out of traffic, which it was very desirable to keep down to a minimum. It was twice converted temporarily to oil burning, during the coal strike of 1921 and again in 1926 (following the general strike of that year). Its number 2290 was changed in September 1947 to 22290, in effect being placed on what was then the 'duplicate' list, owing to the number being acquired by a new 2–6–4T. Under British Railways it received the number 58100 in January 1949, and was painted in the then standard passenger livery for all but top link express engines, this being virtually the old LNWR colours of black lined out in red, cream and grey.

In later days the old lady was usually known affectionately by the nickname of 'Big Bertha' and her ultimate demise in 1956 was a source of general regret by all who had known her.

Some further details of this interesting locomotive would perhaps be of interest, and the following facts and figures have therefore been included:

Driving wheels: 4 ft 7½ in. in diameter
Height to chimney: 13 ft 4 in.
Length (engine only):   35 ft 8½ in.
Maximum width (over cylinders)   8 ft 11¾ in.
Tractive effort: 43,315 lb. at 85 per cent
Boiler pressure: 200 lb. per square inch
Weight in working order: 73.67 tons
Brakes: steam and hand brakes acting on all wheels
Livery (LMS):   unlined black; (BR):   lined black

On a footnote it is worth adding that the engine was also known colloquially as 'Big Emma', although 'Big Bertha' seems to have been the usual appellation.

'9F' 2–10–0s and Other Large Bankers

In continuance of the principle already referred to elsewhere, of maintaining one large engine together with several smaller tank locomotives, only broken by a short period to be mentioned shortly, 'Big Bertha' was replaced by one of the standard BR class '9F' 2–10–0s, one of the most successful of the twelve standard designs that had been adopted for further construction, only to be halted by the abrupt decision to abandon steam working in favour of diesel and electrification.

No. 92079 was the engine allocated to Bromsgrove and it quickly acquired old 2290's electric headlight. It spent several years on the duty, relieved occasionally by other members of the class such as Nos. 92129, 92135, 92223, 92230, 92231 and 92234. These locomotives were, on occasions, used in conjunction with the pannier tanks; on 23rd April, 1964, for example, a diesel-hauled freight train was assisted up the incline by '9F' 2–10–0 No. 92230 and '94XX' 0–6–0PT No. 8402!

In 1949 Gresley's 2–8–8–2 Garratt No. 69999, rendered redundant by the

'Big Bertha', seen at Bromsgrove on 5th June, 1950 in British Railways livery and numbered 58100.   *H.C. Casserley*

'Big Bertha' waits on the up line at Bromsgrove during the 1920s. The 0–10–0 has taken up position at the rear of the train in readiness for the ascent to Blackwell. (The engine has been temporarily fitted with oil burning equipment.)

Oakwood Press Collection

electrification of the Worsborough incline (for which it had been built, in 1925) was sent to Bromsgrove for banking duties, but it never seems to have been very much liked by the Midland men. Nevertheless it spent about a couple of years there before it went back to Mexborough, where it was adapted for oil burning, apparently with the intention of being returned to Bromsgrove. This never happened however, and the engine was scrapped in 1955. It was the most powerful steam locomotive ever to run in the British Isles, and it seems curious that it never attained the same success on Lickey as it had done at Worsborough, and where one would have thought it would have been so suitable.

The Bromsgrove men never liked the Garratt — for one thing it was much harder work in firing with an estimated fuel consumption of 10 to 12 hundredweight for each ascent, compared with the 6–7 hundredweight of 'Big Bertha' and 5 hundredweight with a 'Jinty'. This may have been the reason for the conversion to oil burning, but apparently the idea was dropped after this had been carried out. The engine is mentioned elsewhere in Dr Ransome Wallis's account of his visit in 1950.

Amongst other types that are known to have been used as Lickey bankers there was LNWR 0–8–4T No. 7953, which was tried out in 1929/30, but was not a success. An LMS Garratt, No. 4998, also spent a short time as banker during 1934, while 2290 was away at shops, another experiment which was not repeated. Great Western '52XX' 2–8–0T No. 5226 arrived in May 1958, and apparently came up to expectations as it remained until April 1960. It was a Hereford (85C) engine and was not, officially, transferred to Bromsgrove until November 1959. A '72XX' 2–8–2T, No. 7235, had been tried out on 18th April, 1958 but had to be returned as it was found that it was out of gauge, the cylinders failing to clear the platforms.

With the rapid replacement of steam in the 1960s, diesels inevitably took over the Lickey banking duties, the classes employed being class '37s' and the now-defunct class '35' Hymeks (see below). The last true steam Lickey banker was '9F' 2–10–0 No. 92079, which was still at Bromsgrove in 1962, but although it was one of the few still remaining at the end of the steam era, not being withdrawn from service until 1967, it spent its last few years at Birkenhead.

The LNER Garratt No. 69999 spent a year or two at Bromsgrove after being displaced from the Worsborough Incline. Seen here banking a train near the summit, May 1949.
Oakwood Press Collection

Johnson 0−6−0Ts Nos. 1955 and 1936 stand on the down line at Blackwell in August 1922; both are in unrebuilt condition. *H.C. Casserley*

Johnson 0−6−0Ts Nos. 1936 and 1938 bank an up goods train into Blackwell station in LMS days. The '19XX' 0−6−0Ts worked on the Incline for many years.

H.C. Casserley

Rebuilt Johnson 0–6–0T No. 7235 assists an up passenger working in 1939; these MR tanks were introduced in 1899, and in 1919 the MR started rebuilding them with Belpaire fireboxes – as such they became the prototypes of the familiar LMS standard class 3F tanks.   *E.R. Morten*

Standard LMS class 3F 0–6–0Ts Nos. 47313 and 47425 descend the Incline after assisting an up train on 4th May, 1949.   *H.C. Casserley*

A summary of some of the principal Lickey Incline banking locomotives is given in the following table. The numbers quoted are intended primarily for the benefit of potential modellers, and are not intended to be a complete list of every engine used on the incline; it is hoped, nevertheless, that most of the regular bankers have been listed, and to that extent the numbers quoted are perhaps the most typical.

TYPICAL LICKEY INCLINE BANKERS 1852–1987

Class	Wheelbase	Numbers	Dates
Norris Class A Extra	4–2–0	104/113/114/115	1852
McConnell's Banker	0–6–0WT	105 (later 221)	1853–61
Miscellaneous	0–6–0WT	213A/217/220/223A/322/1092/2016	See text
Johnson class 1	0–6–0T	1932/1933/1934/1935/1936/1937/ 1938/1939/1947/1954/1955	1907–34
Fowler 'Big Bertha'	0–10–0	2290	1920–47
Fowler class 3F	0–6–0	47276/47301/47305/47308/47313/ 47425/47502/47506/47565/47576/ 47623/47635/47638	1948–61
Riddles 9F	2–10–0	92079/92129/92135/92223/92230/ 92231/92234	1956–62
Hawksworth 94XX	0–6–0PT	8400/8401/8402/8403/8404/8405/ 8606/9401/9430/9486/9493	1958–64
Churchward 42XX	2–8–0T	5226	1958–60
Hymek class 35	Bo-Bo	D7011/D7020/D7021/D7022/D7023/ D7024/D7025/D7075/D7095	1967–72
English Electric class 37	Co-Co	37071/37133/37134/37138/37162/ 37230/37251	c.1980

N.B. The dates shown in column 4 relate to the currency of the numbers in the previous column, and are not necessarily the dates at which particular locomotives worked on the incline. The Johnson 0–6–0Ts, for example, were numbered in the 19XX series from 1907 until 1934, after which they were renumbered in the 7200–7259 series to bring them into line with the LMS-built '3F' 0–6–0Ts (which carried on from 7260). In 1948 both of these classes were prefixed by the number '4'. For clarity, only one set of numbers is shown for each class, though it should be stressed that this is an artificial system. Readers wishing for further guidance in relation to the periods at which each class worked on the line should consult the main text.

Some General Comments

Reviewing the period in general, over a century and a half during which the railway has been in operation, so far as the various types of locomotives, aside from the actual bankers already described, it need hardly be said that almost every type of Midland engine, from the days of Kirtley, Johnson, Deeley and Fowler, must have been seen at some time or another, with a few very important and notable exceptions in the pre-grouping era. The famous Johnson/Deeley compounds prior to the grouping were confined entirely to the London–Manchester, Nottingham, Leeds and Carlisle routes and never

A view near the summit in 1911. Johnson 0–6–0T No. 1933 and an unidentified Kirtley straight-framed 0–6–0 assist a northbound passenger train.

Oakwood Collection

Rebuilt Midland 0–6–0Ts Nos. 7236 and 7238 ascend the bank at the rear of an up freight on 29th May, 1935. *H.C. Casserley*

Four standard class 3F 0–6–0Ts descend the Incline in June 1950. No. 47275 is still in LMS livery but No. 47425 sports the earliest BR unlined livery; Nos. 47308 and 47301 carry the British Railways 'unicycling lion' motif. *H.C. Casserley*

worked west of Derby. It was not until after the grouping, when their numbers were considerably increased, that they appeared on the west of England line to Birmingham and Bristol, after which they became a familiar sight until their gradual demise in the 1950s.

The '999' class 4-4-0s would not have been seen as these worked exclusively between Leeds and Carlisle, although No. 995 must have travelled over the line when it was tried out on the Somerset and Dorset in 1924.

The 0-6-0 class '4' goods were similarly unknown at that earlier period; these engines did not start to appear regularly until the later 1920s, but there is in existence an interesting photograph by the late W. Leslie Good, taken at Blackwell on 22nd April, 1922, of MR class '3' goods No. 3604 with a train consisting of the five new class '4' goods built by Armstrong Whitworth & Co. for the Somerset & Dorset (Nos. 57 to 61) en route from the makers to Highbridge, about to descend the incline.

As an afterthought it must be considered very doubtful whether any of the rather short-lived American 2-6-0s ever penetrated this area, an interesting sidelight on the fact that their USA predecessors, the Norris 4-2-0s, made their début so many years before.

Passenger Engines

Prior to the grouping the principal express types were the '700' class Johnson 4-4-0s, working from Derby (none were ever stationed at Bristol), assisted by the rebuilt class '2s', of which Nos. 515-527 were allocated to Bristol, shed 8.

A typical day's observations taken on the occasion of my first visit in August 1916 shows: 2-4-0s, Kirtley double-framed No. 1 class, one (in fact No. 1 itself); Johnson 2-4-0s, four; class '2' 4-4-0s, eight; class '3' 4-4-0s, six; Johnson single-wheelers, two; 0-6-0 Kirtley double-framed, eleven; 0-6-0 Johnson class '2', four; 0-6-0 Johnson class '3', one. This gives a fairly representative picture of the period. The complete absence of tank engines, apart from the bankers themselves, will be noted. There was very little local traffic apart from that to and from Bromsgrove itself. A lot of the traffic from Birmingham at that time went down the Redditch branch from Barnt Green and was handled by 0-4-4Ts and 0-6-4Ts.

However, all the tank classes, including the 0-4-0STs and 0-4-0Ts used for shunting in Gloucester docks, would have been observed on occasions, if only proceeding to or from Derby works.

After the grouping standard LMS types began to make their appearance, notably the Horwich 2-6-0s, and the inevitable Stanier Black Five 4-6-0s — but right up to the end of steam the principal main line expresses were the 'Jubilees', which did magnificent work over the route until their replacement by diesels. Royal Scots and Pacifics, like the compounds before them, never worked between Birmingham and Bristol. Very few 'foreign' types from the LNWR or other associated railways ever made their appearance other than on possible rare occasions, although after 1930 the Somerset &

Dorset 2−8−0s would have been seen from time to time proceeding to or from Derby works for overhaul. Even after the transfer of the whole area to the Western Region in 1958, GWR engines were conspicuous by their absence, owing to clearance restrictions,

Diesel Power on the Lickey

The first diesels to be used on Lickey banking duties were the class '37' Co-Cos, one of the earliest to appear being No. 6938 which was used on an experimental basis in the summer of 1964. On 5th July, 1964 this same engine was noted on the incline in conjunction with a '94XX' 0−6−0PT — an unusual, though by no means unique combination at that time.

Another class '37' used on the incline during the mid-1960s was No. 6977, though in July 1967 the 105 ton Co-Cos were replaced by Hymek class '35s'. In retrospect, these sophisticated diesel-hydraulics were probably ill-suited for use as bankers — they were, for example, much lighter than the class '37s', and weighed only 75 tons. Nevertheless, several Hymeks were allocated to Worcester for use on the incline, the usual practice being for three class '35s' to be used as bankers at any one time. Typical numbers, around 1968, included Nos. D7011, D7020, D7021, D7022, D7023, D7024, D7025, D7075 and D7095.

In general, the late 1960s and early 1970s were a fruitful period for modern traction enthusiasts, and although the majority of express passenger trains were handled by class '47' Co-Cos and class '45' or '46' 1Co-Co1s, a variety of other types also appeared. It was possible, for instance, to see class '52' Western Co-Cos on both passenger and freight duties, while goods workings might produce anything from a '63XX' class '22' Bo-Bo to a class '47'; LMR type 2s were widely used, while class '37s' also appeared regularly. The presence of the class '47s' was perhaps inevitable — and as this versatile class could be seen all over the country it was often viewed as the 'Black Five' of the diesel age! (Class '47s' have also been used on banking duties, albeit on a sporadic basis.)

In recent years the decline in railway freight traffic (and in particular the demise of loose-coupled goods trains) resulted in a decline in the use of bankers on the Lickey Incline. Similarly, the advent of powerful HST sets meant that express passenger trains could surmount the incline without assistance, though it is interesting to recall that, until 1988, a West Country to Scotland sleeper service was regularly banked up the incline. (This service was, in fact, the last remaining passenger train booked for banking assistance on the Lickey Incline.)

Locomotives employed on banking duties in the last few years have usually been class '37s'. These worked in pairs, and engines seen on banking duties have included Nos. 37071, 37133, 37134, 37138, 37162, 37320 and 37251. As mentioned, timetable changes carried out in 1988 brought regular passenger banking to an end, but two class '37s' in multiple are still supplied by Gloucester each weekday night except Saturday. These work at Bromsgrove between about 8.15 pm and 3.30 am (an hour earlier on

Saturday mornings) and have a regular 'clientele' of freight trains requiring their assistance.

As to the future, this important route centred on Birmingham, now the focal point in the Midlands of the British Rail system, remains the vital artery of through communication between the north-east and the south-west, and seems bound to retain its status as one of the principal rail routes not centred on London, or any of the other major cities such as Manchester, Liverpool or Glasgow. Former famous named trains including the 'Pines Express' (now no longer running) and more recently 'The Devonian', which still runs, have been seen on the Lickey Incline over the years, and many through expresses between such centres as Newcastle, Leeds and Sheffield in the North East, and Bristol and the West Country traverse it daily. Although not comparable in speed with the InterCity expresses over the main trunk routes, these nevertheless perform an important function in providing through communication across the country away from London. This is evidenced by the fact that these trains, even during midweek during the least busy periods, are always exceptionally well patronised, often filled to overcrowding. Were it not for the present recession being experienced at the time of writing and cutbacks in capital expenditure, it would even have been possible to forecast eventual electrification, linking up with similar projects which might be envisaged between London, Bristol, etc., which are very much desirable, and which one still hopes might one day come to fruition.

Beyond that it is not possible to forecast the shape of things to come, but one thing is certain, the Lickey Incline, little changed in its essential lay-out since it was built as part of the Birmingham & Gloucester Railway and saw its first train way back in September 1840, will continue into the foreseeable future to function as an essential artery of the network of the British Rail system.

Class 37 No. 37206 (with an up freight train) tops the Lickey Incline on 13th June, 1979, banked by No. 37214 and 37240 of the same class. The steepness of the bank is well shown in this telephoto lens view.   *Brian Morrison*

Class 45/0, No. 45063 near the summit of the Lickey on 21st April, 1979 with the 10.21 Penzance to Bradford Exchange service.   *Brian Morrison*

Climbing the Lickey in September 1982 is class 24 No. 97201 (ex-24,061) with a brake-heat special test train.   *Brian Morrison*

Further Reading

The Lickey Incline has, from time to time, featured in books and articles, and some of these are listed below for the benefit of those seeking further details. It should be noted that most of the following works are out of print — though copies should be available in any good library. For completeness, some articles relating to the types of engine used on the incline have been included.

T.H. Messenger, Memories of the Lickey, *Railway World*, August 1966.
* Bill Ibbott, Big Emma, *Railway Modeller*, October 1967.
* Bill Ibbott, Big Emma's Tender, *Railway Modeller*, November 1967.
  Peter Truman, The Birmingham & Gloucester Railway and the Lickey Incline, *British Railway Journal*, No. 11 1986.
  R.J. Essery, Working On The Lickey, *British Railway Journal*, No. 14 1986.
  Tony Higgs, Last Lickey Bankers, *Railway Magazine*, September 1988.
  J. Glover, Bromsgrove, *Railway Modeller*, May 1973.
  W.J. Gordon, *Everyday Life on the Railroad* (1898).
  C. Hamilton Ellis, *The Midland Railway* (1966).
  Derek G. Pugh, Philosopher Engineer (Herbert Spencer), *Railway Magazine*, June 1986.
* T.A. Lindsay, Midland Railway 0–6–0 Class M, *Model Railway News*, March 1961.
* C.J. Freezer, The Ubiquitous 4F, *Railway Modeller*, November 1964.
* Bill Ibbott & Bob Essery, Ex-Midland 3F 0–6–0, *Railway Modeller*, June 1964.
* Bill Ibbott & Bob Essery, Ex-Midland 3F 0–6–0T, *Railway Modeller*, October 1964.
* Bill Ibbott, The Midland Class 4 Freight, *Railway Modeller*, January 1967.
* Bill Ibbott, Midland Railway 3F 0–6–0T, *Railway Modeller*, March 1967.
* Ian Beattie, LMS class 2P 4–4–0, *Railway Modeller*, December 1984.
* R.J. Essery & G. Toms, The LMS 'Jinties', *British Railway Journal* No. 8 1985.
* Bill Ibbott, Midland 'Spinners', *Railway Modeller*, September 1965.
* Bob Essery, The Garratts, *Railway Modeller*, October 1968.
* Ian Beattie, LNER Garratt, *Railway Modeller*, May 1983.
* Ian Beattie, Fowler 3F Tank, *Railway Modeller*, May 1980.
  C.P. Atkins, More Light on the Lickey Banker, *Back Track*, Summer 1987.
  Bob Danes, Banking After Bertha, *Back Track*, Summer 1987.
  O.S. Nock, Upgrading a Cross-Country Route, *Railway Magazine*, October 1971.
  O.S. Nock, The Bristol–York Route Today, *Railway Magazine*, March 1978.
  Geoffrey Bannister, Summer Saturday on the Lickey, *Railway Magazine*, September 1971.

* = articles containing plans of interest to potential modellers of the Lickey Incline.

Appendix

Extract from Midland Railway 1903 Appendix to the Working Timetable

GENERAL REGULATIONS FOR WORKING THE LICKEY INCLINE, BETWEEN BLACKWELL AND BROMSGROVE.

Descending.

1. The Driver of every Down train must bring his train to a stand at the top of the Incline, and must not proceed with it until he has received permission to do so from the Brakesman, and Brakesmen must, before giving Drivers a signal to descend the Incline, satisfy themselves that these Regulations have been strictly complied with. Drivers of Down Goods and Mineral trains must start at such a speed as will enable the Brakesmen to put down the wagon brakes.

2. No train must leave Blackwell for Bromsgrove with less brake power than shown below :—

All Passenger trains must be worked with the Continuous brake in accordance with the Regulation of Railways Act, 1889 (see pages 198, 199, and 200 of No. 20 Appendix).

In the event of the Continuous brake on a Passenger train requiring to descend the Incline being out of order, the instructions in the following paragraph, respecting Fish, Meat, Fruit, &c., trains must be complied with.

Fish, Meat, Fruit, Milk, Horse, Cattle, or Perishable trains composed of Coaching stock, or Empty Coaching stock trains consisting of more than equal to seven vehicles must have two brakes ; consisting of more than equal to eleven vehicles, three brakes ; and whatever the number of vehicles on the train, at least one vehicle out of every four after the first seven must either be a vehicle fitted with the ordinary hand brake in which a Guard or Brakesman must travel, or a vehicle fitted with a Continuous Brake in use from the engine.

In computing the number of vehicles of a Passenger or Empty Coaching stock train, the instructions on page 219 of No. 20 Appendix must be observed.

The levers of all wagon brakes must be dropped down, and one wagon brake must be pinned down for every two loaded cattle, coal, or heavy loaded goods wagons, and one for every three empty wagons or lightly loaded goods wagons.

3. The Brakesmen must be careful to ascertain that the brakes pinned down are in good order, and they must increase the brake power beyond what is above stated should they consider it necessary to do so, in consequence of the state of the weather, or from any other cause, and, when necessary, the Incline brakes provided for the purpose must be used, at the discretion of the Brakesmen. Brakesmen need not accompany trains down the Incline, except when the number of Guards is not sufficient to apply the prescribed number of hand brakes, or when Incline brakes are used.

4. Guards must apply the ordinary hand brakes when descending the Incline, whether the vehicles in which they are travelling are fitted with a Continuous brake in use from the engine or not.

5. Passenger trains must not descend the Incline in less than five minutes, or at a greater speed than twenty-seven miles per hour, and Goods trains in less than twelve minutes, or at a greater speed than eleven miles per hour.

6. Down Passenger trains not booked to stop at Bromsgrove must run on the down middle line between the platforms, and Drivers must, after satisfying themselves that their brakes are in good working order, reduce the speed of their trains so as to pass over the down middle line at a speed not exceeding 10 MILES PER HOUR.

All Down Passenger trains booked to stop at Bromsgrove for traffic purposes must be brought to a stand at the down platform.

All Down Goods and Mineral trains must be brought to a stand between the Passenger Station and the South Box with the rear vehicle clear of the connection between the down platform line and the down passenger line at the Bristol end of the Station. In the event of a Down Goods or Mineral train being brought to a stand before the rear vehicle is clear of the connection between the down platform line and the down passenger line at the Bristol end of the Station, it must be drawn clear of that connection before the engine is uncoupled, or any vehicle is attached or detached. On arrival at Bromsgrove, any brakes that may have been applied, must be released, unless it is necessary for them to remain on for any purpose. Drivers must not proceed, after their trains have been brought to a stand, until they have obtained the usual signal from the Guard to do so.

7. In accordance with Clause 13 of these Regulations, bank engines may, after having been brought to a stand, and the Drivers cautioned, either ver; ally or by hand lamp or flag. as to the obstruction before them, be allowed to proceed from Blackwell to Bromsgrove Station when a light engine or train, other than a Passenger train, is on the down main line in the section between Blackwell and Bromsgrove Stati n ; and in accordance with Clause 14 of these Regulations, bank engines may, after having been brought to a stand, and the Drivers cautioned, either verbally or by hand lamp or flag. as to the obstruction before them, be allowed to proceed from Bromsgrove Station to Bromsgrove South Box on the down passenger or down goods line when a Down light engine or train, other than a Passenger train, is in the section between Bromsgrove Station and Bromsgrove South Box on the line on which the bank engines require to run.

Ascending.

8. All Up trains requiring assistance must be brought to a stand at Bromsgrove.
9. No train must ascend the Incline without an assistant engine being immediately behind the last vehicle, except Passenger trains formed of not more than equal to six vehicles ; Mineral trains of not more than eight wagons ; Goods trains of not more than ten wagons ; and Empty Wagon trains of not more than fifteen wagons, which can go up the Incline unassisted by a bank engine, provided the last vehicle is a brake-van with a Guard in charge.
10. When an Up-Passenger train not booked to stop at Blackwell is required to stop at that station for traffic purposes, the Signalman at Blackwell must be specially instructed to keep his signals at Danger until the train is near to the home signal. and the Driver of the bank engine assisting the train must be advised before leaving Bromsgrove that the train has to stop at Blackwell. The Station-masters at Bromsgrove and Blackwell will be informed of such extra stops, and the Bromsgrove Station-master will be held responsible for advising the Driver of the bank engine, and the Blackwell Station-master for advising the Signalman at that Station.

Special Instructions respecting the Signalling of Down Trains and Engines.

11. Except as provided in Clause 12 of the Regulations for the signalling of bank engines the Signalman at the Bromsgrove Station Box must not give permission on the Block Telegraph for a Down train or engine to leave Blackwell when any obstruction exists on the down main line, or on the down platform line on the Blackwell side of the connection from the down platform line to the down passenger line on the Bristol side of the Station, or on the line on which the train or engine requires to run on the Blackwell side of the Bromsgrove South Box, nor until permission has been obtained on the Block Telegraph for the train or engine to proceed to the South Box on the line on which it requires to run, and the Facing Points have been set for that line.
12. The Signalman at Bromsgrove Station Box may, in Clear Weather, give permission on the Block Telegraph, in accordance with the " Section Clear but Station or Junction Blocked " signal (Warning Arrangement), for a bank engine to leave Blackwell before permission has been obtained on the Block Telegraph for the bank engine to proceed to Bromsgr. e South Box, providing the down main and down platform lines through the Station are clear, that the " Train out of Section " signal has been received from the Bromsgrove South Box for the previous train or engine passing over the line for which the facing points are set, and that line is clear to the Bromsgrove South Box down home signal.

The Signalman at Blackwell must be extremely careful not to allow any train or engine other than an engine regularly in use between Blackwell and Bromsgrove as a bank engine to proceed towards Bromsgrove Station Box under the " Section Clear but Station or Junction Blocked " signal (Warning Arrangement).
13. The Signalman at Bromsgrove South Box must not give permission on the Block Telegraph for a down train or engine to approach when any obstruction exists on the Bromsgrove side of his up distant signal, on the line on which the train or engine requires to run, nor until all the points over which it has to pass have been placed in the proper position for the train or engine to proceed towards Stoke Works.

14. The Signalman at Blackwell may, when necessary, allow one or more bank engines to proceed from Blackwell to Bromsgrove on the down main line during the time a light engine or train, other than a Passenger train, is in the section, after the " Train entering Section " Bell signal has been given and acknowledged for each engine, and the Driver has been cautioned, either verbally or by hand lamp or flag, as to the obstruction before him, and the Signalmen at Blackwell and Bromsgrove Station Boxes must make a note in their Train Register Books of each engine so signalled. The Signalman at the Bromsgrove Station Box must not give the " Train out of Section " signal to Blackwell until the last engine so signalled has passed his Post, when he will call the attention of, and give the " Train out of Section " signal to the Signalman at Blackwell for the train, and for each engine that has been allowed to follow it in accordance with these Regulations, and the Signalman at Blackwell must acknowledge each " Train out of Section " signal so given. The Signalman at Blackwell must take care to obtain the " Train out of Section " signal for the train, and for each engine that has been allowed to follow it, and enter such signals in his Train Register Book before giving the " Is Line Clear? " signals for any other Down train or engine to proceed from Blackwell to Bromsgrove.

After a Down Passenger train has been allowed to leave Blackwell, no bank engine going towards Bromsgrove must be allowed to enter the section until the " Train out of Section " signal has been received from Bromsgrove Station Box for the Passenger train, and permission has been obtained on the Block Telegraph for the bank engine to proceed to Bromsgrove.

15. The Signalman at Bromsgrove Station Box may, when necessary, allow one or more bank engines to proceed from Bromsgrove Station to Bromsgrove South Box on the down passenger or down goods line, during the time a light engine or train, other than a Passenger train, is in the section, but before any bank engine is allowed to proceed to the Bromsgrove South Box during the time a light engine or train, other than a Passenger train, is in the section, the " Train entering Section " Bell signal must be given and acknowledged for each engine, and each engine must be brought TO A STAND, and the Driver cautioned, either verbally or by hand lamp or flag, as to the obstruction before him, and the Signalmen at Bromsgrove Station and South Boxes must make a note in their Train Register Books of each engine so signalled. The Signalman at the Bromsgrove South Box must not give the " Train out of Section " signal to the Signalman at Bromsgrove Station Box until the last engine so signalled has passed his Post, when he will call the attention of, and give the " Train out of Section " signal to the Signalman at Bromsgrove Station Box for the train, and for each engine that has been allowed to follow it in accordance with these Regulations, and the Signalman at Bromsgrove Station Box must acknowledge each " Train out of Section " signal so given. The Signalman at Bromsgrove Station Box must take care to obtain the " Train out of Section " signal for the train, and for each engine that has been allowed to follow it, and enter such signals in his Train Register Book before giving the " Is Line Clear? " signals for any other Down train or engine to proceed from Bromsgrove Station to Bromsgrove South Box on the same line.

After a Down Passenger train has been allowed to leave Bromsgrove Station Box, no bank engine going towards Bromsgrove South Box must be allowed to enter the section until the " Train out of Section " signal has been received from Bromsgrove South Box for the Passenger train, and permission has been obtained on the Block Telegraph for the bank engine to proceed to Bromsgrove South Box.

Regulations for working the Incline in the event of the failure of the Block Telegraph Instruments or Bells.

16. In the event of any failure of the Block Telegraph Instruments or Bells applicable to the down main line between Blackwell and Bromsgrove Stations, so that the necessary signals cannot be forwarded and received, the traffic on the down main line must be worked by a Pilotman appointed by the Station-master at Bromsgrove.

The Pilotman must wear the distinctive badge prescribed in Rule 227 in the Company's Book of Rules and Regulations, and must accompany every train or engine from Blackwell to Bromsgrove. Two or more engines may be coupled together, but they must not be uncoupled until brought to a stand at Bromsgrove Station.

Three of the printed forms provided for the purpose must be filled up and signed by the Station-master at Bromsgrove ; one of these he must deliver to the Signalman at the Bromsgrove Station Box, and one to the Signalman at Blackwell, the signature of each Signalman being obtained on the third form, which the Station-master at Bromsgrove must hand to the Pilotman, and obtain his signature to it also.

The Pilotman must not leave Bromsgrove Station Signal Box until the down platform line and the down main line are clear through Bromsgrove Station, and permission has been obtained on the Block Telegraph for the next train or engine from Blackwell to proceed to the South Box, and the points are open for the line on which the train or engine is required to run. During the absence of the Pilotman no obstruction of either of the down lines must be allowed, and the points must not be moved.

17. In the event of any failure of the Block Telegraph Instruments or Bells applicable to the down passenger line or to the down goods line between Bromsgrove Station and Bromsgrove South Box, at the same time that a failure of the Instruments or Bells applicable to the down main line between Blackwell and Bromsgrove exists, the traffic from Blackwell to Bromsgrove Station on the down main line, and from Bromsgrove Station to the South Box on the down passenger and down goods lines must be worked by a Pilotman appointed by the Station-master at Bromsgrove.

The Pilotman must wear the distinctive Badge prescribed in Rule 227 in the Company's Book of Rules and Regulations, and must accompany every train or engine from Blackwell to Bromsgrove Station, and every train or engine from Bromsgrove Station to Bromsgrove South Box. Two or more engines may be coupled together, but they must not be uncoupled until brought to a stand at Bromsgrove Station or Bromsgrove South Box, as the case may be.

Four of the printed forms provided for the purpose must be filled up and signed by the Station-master at Bromsgrove ; one of these he must deliver to the Signalman at the Bromsgrove South Box, one to the Signalman at the Bromsgrove Station Box, and one to the Signalman at Blackwell, the signature of each of the Signalmen being obtained on the fourth form, which the Station-master at Bromsgrove must hand to the Pilotman and obtain his signature to it also.

The Pilotman must not leave Bromsgrove until the down platform line and the down main line are clear through Bromsgrove Station, and the line on which the train or engine is required to run beyond the Station is clear to the up distant signal worked from Bromsgrove South Box, and all the points are open for that line. During the absence of the Pilotman, no obstruction of either of the down lines through the Station, or of the line on which the train or engine is required to run beyond the Station must be allowed, and the points must not be moved.

18. During the absence from Blackwell of the Pilotman, no obstruction of the down main line on the Bromsgrove Station side of the Blackwell down home signal must be allowed.

19. If the pilot engine is required to assist a train from Bromsgrove to Blackwell on the up main line, the Pilotman may return to Blackwell on that line.

20. When the failure of the Block Telegraph Instruments or Bells has been repaired, and they are again in good working order, the Pilotman must, on accompanying the last train or engine allowed to proceed under these Regulations, withdraw the forms above-mentioned, by a written order from the Station-master at Bromsgrove, nd the Signalman at the Bromsgrove Station Box in the case of a failure between Blackwell and Bromsgrove Station Box, and the Signalmen at the Bromsgrove Station and South Boxes in the case of a failure between Blackwell and Bromsgrove South Box must, on receipt of the order cancelling the working by Pilotman, give the " Train out of Section " signal to the Signal Box in the rear, and the signalling must then be recommenced in accordance' with the Block Telegraph Regulations and the Special Instructions issued to the Signalmen. The forms which have been issued must be collected and sent to the District Superintendent.

21. In the event of any failure of the Block Telegraph Instruments or Bells so that the necessary signals cannot be forwarded and received for the down passenger line, or for the down goods line, from the Bromsgrove Station Box to the South Box, and the Block Telegraph Instruments and Bells between Blackwell and Bromsgrove Station are in working order, the traffic on the down lines through Bromsgrove Station to the South Box must be worked by a Pilotman appointed by the Station-master at Bromsgrove.

The Pilotman must wear the distinctive Badge prescribed in Rule 227 in the Company's Book of Rules and Regulations, and the Signalman at the Bromsgrove Station Box must not give permission on the Block Telegraph for any train or engine to leave Blackwell until he has ascertained by sending the Pilotman to the South Box, that the line on which the train or engine requires to run is clear to the distant signal for the up line worked from the South Box, that all the points are open for the line on which the train or engine requires to run, and that the Signalman at the South Box will keep the line clear and not move the points until the train or engine from Blackwell has arrived.

Three of the printed forms provided for the purpose must be filled up and signed by the Station-master at Bromsgrove; one of these he must deliver to the Signalman at the South Box, and one to the Signalman at the Station Box, the signature of each Signalman being obtained on the third form, which the Station-master at Bromsgrove must hand to the Pilotman and obtain his signature to it also.

When the failure of the Block Telegraph Instruments or Bells has been repaired and they are again in good working order, the Pilotman must withdraw the forms above mentioned by a written order from the Station-master at Bromsgrove, and the Signalman at the Bromsgrove South Box must, on receipt of the order cancelling the working by Pilotman, give the "Train out of Section" signal · to the Bromsgrove Station Box, and the signalling must then be recommenced in accordance with the Block Telegraph Regulations, and the Special Instructions issued to the Signalmen. The forms which have been issued must be collected and sent to the District Superintendent.

22. In the event of any failure of the Block Telegraph Instruments or Bells for the up passenger or the up goods line from Bromsgrove South Box to the Station Box, or for the up main line from Bromsgrove Station Box to Blackwell, so that the necessary signals cannot be forwarded and received, the instructions contained in Rule 25 of the Block Telegraph Regulations, or Rule 25 of the General Regulations for Train Signalling by Telegraph Bells, as the case may be, must be strictly carried out.

23. The Station-master at Blackwell and the Station-master and Loco. Foreman at Bromsgrove will be held responsible for taking care that these Regulations are strictly carried out, and should any breach of them occur, it must be immediately reported to the Superintendent of the Line and the District Superintendent.

A Great Western '94XX' 0–6–0PT No. 8400 banks a northbound passenger train up the Incline on 23rd April, 1958.   *R.M. Casserley*

'Big Bertha' banks an up goods working at the top of the Incline; bankers were never coupled to the trains being assisted, and this enabled them to drop behind the assisted train at Blackwell.   *H.C. Casserley*

Seen here at Bromsgrove coaling stage on 6th January, 1957, class 9F 2–10–0, No. 92079 awaits with full head of steam for her next duty. Note the headlight fitted to this locomotive.   *H.C. Casserley*